Presence

"A clear, wise, and sometimes provocative description of the Buddha's path through a contemporary landscape."

— ***Delson Armstrong****, author of* A Mind Without Craving

"Through over fifty years of training and practice, Doug Kraft has delved deeply into traditional Buddhism. As a psychotherapist, meditation teacher, and minister, he has integrated these teachings into everyday life. In this book, he uses emerging neuroscience findings to enhance our meditation techniques and uses Buddhism to illuminate the science. Weaving them together with stories makes it all an easy read. He has gone far and brings us along with him."

— ***John Travis****, senior Dharma teacher emeritus at Spirit Rock Meditation Center*

"Doug offers a skillful synthesis of modern science and meditation. Theoretical, practical, experiential — it's all in here with relatable examples, clear language, and a fair share of 'oh wow' dots connected. All the while, it brought me into the present. For those looking to deepen their wisdom while nurturing their intellect, I highly recommend this book."

— ***Liam McClintock****, founder of FitMind*

"Doug Kraft, the noted meditation teacher and author of *Buddha's Map*, takes a fascinating dive into the connection between neuroscience and awakening. Through stories and engaging personal anecdotes, Doug explains what scientists have discovered and confirms what the Buddha taught 2,600 years ago."

— ***David Johnson****, author of* Path to Nibbāna

also by Doug Kraft

Centering Home

Buddha's Map

Beginning the Journey

Kindness and Wisdom Practice

Meditator's Field Guide

Befriending the Mind

Resting in the Waves

Presence:

Quiet Awareness and How It Emerges in Meditation and the Brain

Doug Kraft

Easing Awake Books

Published by Easing Awake Books, 2023
Carmichael, CA 95608
https://www.easingawake.com
March 5, 2023

ISBN: 978-1-7350737-2-9 paperback
ISBN: 978-1-7350737-3-6 e-book

Unless noted otherwise, *sutta* translations are from Bhikkhu Bodhi through Wisdom Publications (199 Elm Street, Somerville, MA 02144).

I am grateful for the following www.unsplash.com photos:
- Twilight photo on the cover
- Two Path on page 3 by Jens Lelie
- Roots on page 11 by Jeremy Bishop
- River on page 35 by Jack Anstey
- Buddha on page 59 by Jan Kopfiva
- Tree in Pond on page 69 by Gaye Cornish
- Squirrel on page 89 by Georg Eiermann
- Woman on page 121 by Danie Franco
- Bird on page 138 by Svetizar Cenisev
- Greedy Squirrel on page 139 by Muhil Mohan
- Raccoon on page 140 by Yannick Menard
- Rat on page 141 by Alexandr Gusev
- Rat on page 143 by Joshua J Cotton
- Leap on page 157 by Kid Circus
- Swirls on page 167 by Daniel Levis Pelusion
- Tangle on page 179 by Kier In Sight
- Mirror Shadow on page 199 by Mateus Campos Felipe
- Twilight photo on page 213 by Guillame Briard

Printed in the United States
5 4 3 2 1

Knowing that one day this body will cease,
I seek simplicity, clarity, and kindness.

When sending and receiving kindness feel the same,
self dissolves into contentment,
yearning fades into timeless presence,
and eternity merges with this moment right now.

Contents

Appendices

1

Introduction: Emerging Clear Awareness

Presence

What are you aware of right now?

Presence means being aware of the moment with undivided attention. Some people think that to be present, we have to shut out all but one thing at a time. Instead, I'll be advocating a wide-open presence. Such relaxed awareness may include many things at once. For me, presence means being with life as it is in all its fullness.

When the word "presence" stands alone, it can be both a means and an end. Many spiritual and psychological traditions advocate presence as a means of cultivating wellbeing. It is a tool or a technique meant to get us somewhere. But presence can also be an end in itself — a description of what it's like to be content with life as it is. It can be a place where we arrive when we are truly right here.

When I sit in meditation, watching my mind-heart drift hither and yon, presence both reminds me to be aware of the current moment and brings me there all at the same time. And it bypasses the need to conjure up a sense of a "self" that is doing it all. Rather than feeling, "I am present," there is just presence.

To be clear, presence is not a thing that can be known. But it is the space within which things can be known. It's like outer space. On a clear night we can gaze out into infinity. "Outer space" is not the stars or planets or derelict satellites. It is the space that encompasses all those objects, large and small. It is not a thing, but without space to hold things there cannot be anything. Without inner space, or consciousness, we cannot know anything.

A synonym for presence is "clear awareness." Without some presence, nothing can be known.

Emerging Clear Awareness

The word "emerging" in that phrase can be a verb or a modifier or both. As a verb it's about clear awareness coming forth. Perhaps something can help it along. As a modifier it describes an aspect of clear awareness. And as before, the phrase doesn't require a subject — a self — that is doing or modifying the emerging.

My mind works visually. When I think "emerging clear awareness," I imagine a clear sky at twilight, like the cover of this book. The sun is out of sight, just below the horizon, even as it sends light into the visible sky. And there is also a hint of vast emptiness — like what we see gazing into a moonless night. In the twilight image, it is unclear whether the sun is rising or setting, whether it's dawn or dusk. A simple way to describe that feeling is "presence: emerging clear awareness."

It will become apparent in the coming pages that as awareness gets clearer and clearer, there comes a moment when it fades into cessation (*nirodha* in Pāli, the language of the Buddhist text) and extinction (*nibbāna*).

Weaving the Two Paths Together

Throughout this book, we'll be fleshing out these metaphors beginning with the questions "What are consciousness and clear awareness?" and "How do they work?" as well as "How do they relate to presence, inner peace, and wellbeing?"

I've been intrigued by these questions since I was a child trying to imagine viewing the world through the eyes of my cat or a bird or my friend, Rex, down the street. Six decades later, these questions still underlie my deepest yearnings.

While I don't have definitive answers, I have wandered down enough dead ends to be able to confidently eliminate some paths. What I have found is two paths to understanding consciousness and presence, paths that are illuminating and offer great promise. They are:

- The Buddha's simple, original teachings
- The neuroscience of the brain in general and homeostatic balancing in particular

I know, those paths seem incompatible. For one thing, they employ very different vocabularies. Buddhist meditation speaks about mindfulness, awareness, *sati, mettā, sampajañña, jhānas,* nirodha, nibbāna, and more. Neuroscience talks about neurons, myelin sheathing, the brain, error correction, Bayesian inference, amygdala, neocortex, periaqueduct gray (PAG), and more. The neuroscience of the brain and the path of meditation sound like different galaxies.

But as I began to comprehend what brain research has discovered in the last fifty years, I started to see these findings reflected in my meditation, even though the language and concepts were alien to my training. Indeed, from their scientific writings, I couldn't tell whether or not the researchers had regular contemplative practices themselves. But bit by bit I could see in my practice what they were talking about. It clarified many aspects of my experience. Comparing technical understanding of the brain to the Buddha's understanding of the mind was complicated. But when I found connections, my meditation deepened and took me to places I had not thought possible. Gradually I was convinced these two paths were looking at the same experiences but through very different lenses. The Buddha looked from inside experience. Neuroscience looks from the outside. However, the actual phenomena has more in common than was apparent at first glance.

For example, a careful reading of the Buddha's teachings suggests that part of spiritual practice involves eliminating greed, hatred, and delusion. He never said it means getting rid of pain and pleasure. Those are wired into us. We can't control what we feel. But we do have some influence over how we respond: we don't have to grab hold of pleasure or push away pain.

So his First Noble Truth is not about eliminating suffering. It is about *understanding* how it operates. This understanding reveals that the core of suffering is tension (*taṇhā*). The Second Noble Truth is about allowing that tension to subside. This leads to the Third Noble Truth, which has to do with realizing a deep sense of peace and wellbeing (nirodha).

Meanwhile neuroscience talks about homeostatic variables such as body temperature, blood oxygen, hydration, rest, social contact, and much more. These variables must be kept within narrow ranges or we get sick or die. When a homeostatic variable goes out of its optimal range, we feel bad and suffer. When it comes back into balance, we feel good. So pain and pleasure give us a reading on how healthy our system is and motivate us to take corrective action (e.g., putting on a warm jacket, drinking, resting, eating) to bring us back into healthy equilibrium. Pain and pleasure are vital signals that help us self-regulate.

Thus, the Buddha's Noble Truths and the concept of homeostasis are pointing to the same phenomena. The language, points of view, and conceptual frameworks are different, but what we do about it is the same, whether we are a good student of the Buddha or a good student of neuroscience and homeostasis.

Most of us view the world through two eyes. Each eye has a slightly different image of the same landscape. The subtle differences allow us to discern depth. Once we realize that the Buddha and biological science are looking at the same world through the same brain, we are able to perceive with greater depth and wisdom.

Therefore, in the coming pages we will explore presence, consciousness, and awareness by alternating between these two perspectives. We will shift back and forth in order to get a fuller and more nuanced understanding than is possible through a singular point of view.

Consciousness, World, and Self

We'll start in Chapter 2 with primordial affective emotions because they play an outsized role in our wellbeing. Without them there is no clear awareness, no consciousness, no presence, nothing.

All emotions have several components which may include affect (subjective feelings), cognition (thoughts, expectations), expressions (gestures), motivations (tendencies to act), and physiological changes (heart rates, breath rates, neurological firing). In addition, primordial affective emotions are wired into the brain itself.

When affective emotions are active, we have normal consciousness, including monkey-mind and all the rest. When they are active but quiescent, we are clear, conscious, and at peace with the world. The present moment becomes quietly luminous. Working wisely and kindly with the affective emotions puts us in touch with some of the roots of consciousness and wellbeing. Even if it's difficult and seemingly complicated at first, the payoff is enormous.

Chapters 3 through 6 explore what happens when affective emotions are alive and working smoothly, and how to bring them back to quiescence when they have run off.

Subsequent chapters follow a similar pattern of weaving back and forth between the Buddha's insights and neuroscientific discoveries as we explore other topics. Those topics are grouped into three larger sections:

• ***Constructing a Consciousness*** — as outlined above (Chapters 2 through 6), including the special role of homeostasis and complexity in birthing consciousness (Chapters 7 and 8)

• ***Constructing a World*** — the way consciousness builds a model of what's out there in the world using guesswork (Chapters 9 and 10)

• ***Constructing a Self*** — the way consciousness creates a sense of self out of thin air (Chapters 11 through 14)

When all those topics are resolved and relaxed, they leave behind an abiding and sometimes enigmatic sense of *presence*.

Constructing a Consciousness

2

The Roots of Consciousness: The Primordial Affective Emotions

How does consciousness arise? What is it made of? What are its ingredients? The Buddha combined these into a single question: "What are the causes and conditions that give rise to consciousness?"

Neural science has demonstrated that one necessary condition is affective emotions. Of all the roots of consciousness, the affective emotions are unique in that they can be known directly through introspection. This makes them a powerful tool for deepening and quieting the mind. But first we have to learn to recognize them in our own experience. That is the subject of this chapter.

Affective emotions arise from inside the body and give us a measure of how well or how poorly our life is going. If I ask you "What's going on inside?" you probably won't tell me about your liver, spleen, or hip joints. You'll tell me how good or bad you feel about the course of your life at the moment.

Those are primordial affective emotions. They are completely, 100 percent subjective. We can't measure them objectively with a ruler, photometer, or audio monitor. We can only know them from inside ourselves. I can't feel your affective emotions and you can't feel mine.

By your facial expressions I may infer how you are doing. I know that when I smile, it's usually because I'm feeling good. So, if I see you smiling, I infer you're doing well. But even if I have great empathy and can read the subtlest of clues, it's still only a guess. Sometimes I'm wrong. You might be smiling because you feel embarrassed by my question. A baby may smile because of stomach gas.

Despite the difficulties of measuring affective emotions objectively, in the last half century scientists have been able to glean a lot of objective information about how they work in the brain.[1]

The first thing they found is that affective emotions are hardwired into the lower parts of the brain by the forces of evolution. I had always thought consciousness was a higher brain function that came out of the cerebral cortex. This is where we think, cogitate, and ponder. In contrast, the mid and lower brain are more primitive and earlier in evolution.

For example, one of the affective emotions is rage. Part of the rage circuitry in the midbrain runs from the periaqueductal gray (PAG), which is right in the center of the midbrain and

---

[1] Jaak Panksepp was among the first scientists to map out the affective emotions (Panksepp and Biven, *The Archaeology of Mind)*. Mark Solms gives a comprehensive, well-written overview (Solms, *The Hidden Spring)*.

goes to the medial hypothalamus.[2] If we insert an electrode into this circuitry in a cat and deliver a small electric shock, the cat will go instantly from a quiet purr to a full-blown, fang-exposed, claws-extended, hissing rage. On the other hand, if we insert a tiny scalpel into this circuitry and destroy it, there is nothing we can do to the cat to elicit anger.

Rage is one of seven affective emotions that have distinctive subcortical circuitry. If we take out all seven by anesthetizing or cutting specific, tiny subcortical areas, the creature drops into a coma. Without affective emotions, there is no consciousness whatsoever. It's gone.[3]

In contrast, if we remove the entire neocortex, people and mammals can do surprisingly well. For example, Jaak Panksepp surgically removed the neocortex from a rat. He had sixteen graduate students observe the rat along with a second rat that had a neocortex. Panksepp asked the students to figure out which rat had a full brain.

Twelve of the sixteen students — 75 percent — mistakenly said the decorticated rat was the one with all its gray matter. Apparently, this was because the fully intact creature cowered in its cage while the decorticated rodent explored, preened, cared for others, played, and more. The cowering rats appeared to be stupid from the students' perspective.[4]

---

[2] Panksepp and Biven, p. 18.

[3] So far as I know, no one has actually taken out these sever areas in a human. The ethical objections to such a procedure are obvious and overwhelming. However, all mammals share these seven specific areas. Some researchers have destroyed these in nonhuman mammals. The results have always been complete unconsciousness. And there are rare cases in humans where these areas have been partially or totally removed through accident or disease. The results have been consistent (though not 100 percent conclusive) with the hypothesis that without these areas intact, there is comma. *Ibid.*

[4] Solms, pp. 51-77.

Again, so far as I know, no one has decorticated a human. But there are rare cases of children born without a neocortex. Usually there had been a stroke in utero that blocked blood flow to the neocortex of the fetus so that it died or never developed. This condition is called "hydrocephalus" because there is cerebrospinal fluid where the neocortex is supposed to be.

Hydrocephalic children don't have real speech and do have other disabilities. But they can be curious, laugh, express fear, learn from experience, develop preferences, play, and so forth. They are conscious.

To be sure, in mammals and birds the neocortex interacts with affective emotions to enhance, suppress, modify, and otherwise shape them and give rise to other secondary and tertiary emotions. But even without these interactions, the creature can be fully conscious. However, without the subcortical affective emotions, creatures usually remain in a coma. Affective emotions are among the substantive roots of consciousness.

So I'd like to explore affective emotions, how to recognize them, and how relating to them wisely can deepen our meditation practice and enrich our lives.

Despite their subjective characteristics, seven distinct affective emotions have been identified and studied extensively. Scientists have mapped out where they are in the subcortex and how they connect to other parts of the nervous system. The interactions are so extensive that they do not operate in isolation. They connect in an interdependent network. However, for the purpose of elucidation, we can describe them separately.

Jaak Panksepp[5] gives them seven common names but capitalizes them to remind us that he is referring to a more precise scientific description.

These affective emotions have been bred into us by the forces of evolution. They motivate us to do something. The seven are listed below in their probable evolutionary order along with their names and some of the feelings associated with each:

- SEEKING / Expectancy
- RAGE / Anger
- FEAR / Anxiety
- LUST / Sexual Feelings
- CARE / Nurturing
- CONNECTION / Panic and Grief
- PLAY / Joy and "Lovable Oddity"

While these seven have been studied by scientists, they have not been explored as much by meditators. So I want to look at these not only through the eyes of science and evolution, but also through Buddhist eyes to see how they can inform our practice.

I have found affective emotions can be a practical help in deepening meditation practice. When I recognize any one of the seven in meditation and turn toward and relax into it, the mind tends to quiet down more quickly.

Affective emotions often undergird the thoughts, stories, and other hindrances that arise in meditation. Relaxing into them often moves us toward cessation — what the Buddha called "nirodha." These seven affective emotions also offer insights into selflessness, peace, and impersonal wellbeing.

---

[5] *Ibid,* Panksepp and Biven.

This is partly what the Buddha meant by the Dhammā teachings being "good in the beginning."

SEEKING/Expectancy

SEEKING is the first primary emotion. It is often accompanied by the emotional tones of expectancy, curiosity, or interest. It is the most generalized and probably the oldest in evolutionary terms.

When a mammal or bird sees something unusual in their surroundings, their attention is drawn to it. A little dopamine is secreted into the brain, giving a slightly elevated mood that motivates the creature to find out more about what's going on. There is a little of this seeking in most of the primary emotions.

One common feeling tone is curiosity. However, the tone is not always positive. If we're in a burning building that is running out of oxygen, we will seek a safe exit. If we're hungry, rather than sitting around and brooding, we feel the urge to find something to eat. This is "seeking behavior," but it has more urgency than we associate with mere curiosity.

SEEKING can motivate us to find specific resources. It can also motivate us to just get to know the neighborhood. From an evolutionary perspective, we gain knowledge of the landscape that may help us later when a particular need arises.

These days advertisers and high-tech companies are uncovering specific triggers for SEEKING and building them into sales pitches and search algorithms. If you find yourself surfing the Internet more than you'd like, it may be because engineers have wittingly or unwittingly found ways to trigger this primary affective emotion.

From a meditative perspective, SEEKING can help or hinder our practice. It can motivate us to seek teachings, learn techniques, find supportive *saṅghas*, and more. But as meditation deepens, it is more skillful to sit back and see what arises rather than always looking down the road or around the next bend. As our practice gets subtler, it helps to receive the moment with open awareness rather than being filled with expectations. SEEKING can become a hindrance that stirs the mind up rather than helping it to settle.

In this situation, it is wise to use the Six Rs (Recognize, Release, Relax, Re-Smile, Return, and Repeat), or more simply to turn toward, relax into, and savor / smile. (See note below on the Six Rs and Three Practices.)

Hindrances are always accompanied by tension. So, it helps to recognize any tightness inherent in seeking and let it relax or soften.

Trying to push SEEKING away is fraught with difficulty. It is wired into us and may arise whether we want it or not. So, in the long run, it is always better to utilize relaxed awareness to recognize what is going on, to smile, and to allow the tension to dissolve in the light of that awareness.

Note on the Six Rs and Three Practices

If you are not familiar with the ***Six Rs*** and would like to deepen your meditation, they are a highly effective way to respond to the inevitable hindrances and distractions that come into meditation and life. You can find a full description in the appendices of this book (pp. 225-229).

As you become proficient with them, they may consolidate into the ***Three Ennobling Practices*** (or "***Three Practices***" for short). These are based on the instructions given by the Buddha in the first three of the Four Noble Truths (see Chapter 5). The phrase "turn toward, relax into, and savor / smile" is a reminder of these three. For the sake of literary simplicity, I sometimes shorten the phrase. But a full practice uses all three. They inject kindness, wisdom, and ease into meditation.

RAGE/Anger

RAGE is the second primary affective emotion. A perceived threat triggers this circuitry: perhaps a dog threatened your child or someone cuts you off on the highway or you get passed over for a deserved raise. Its evolutionary advantage is obvious: it motivates us to defend ourselves or loved ones from potential damage. Its disadvantage may be obvious as well: there are many situations for which full-blown RAGE may be understandable but not helpful.

This circuitry evolved over hundreds of generations whereas the circumstances of our lives may evolve in a few moments. A wired-in instinct may not adapt quickly to a rapidly changing environment. It's a blunt-force emotion whereas the situations in our lives may require nuance. If we fly into a tantrum with every hint of ego bruising, we may make our lives miserable — not to mention the lives those around us.

Fortunately, the neocortex can make rapid and nuanced assessments of our situation and what's needed. It can work closely with primary emotions such as RAGE to modify or adapt a course of action. So, rather than express raw RAGE, we can sometimes just feel the anger, annoyance, or peevishness and relax into it or adjust our actions in other ways.

If we have recurring anger, guilt, shame, or embarrassment, there are a few other considerations that may help. One is to see if we are responding adequately to a legitimate physical, social, or mental threat. The circuitry for RAGE is wired in and will continue to be triggered if there is real danger. Without resolving that threat, it's difficult to relax the RAGE.

But if there is no actual danger and the feelings continue, it is helpful to shift attention from the content of the mind (the stories and rationale) to the processes and feelings themselves: thinking, worrying, complaining, and so forth. Stories and thoughts can spin off into the past and future. But our mental processes are always in the present. When we open to them, they often shift on their own.

With greater perspective, we might see that the person or people who occasioned our rage are themselves out of balance and hurting. This recognition might evoke compassion in us for their plight, which in some situations is a healthy and healing response.

However, it can be unhealthy if we think something is wrong with us for feeling anger in the first place. Some religious and meditative communities believe it is wrong to feel aggression. This belief may give rise to guilt, embarrassment, shame, and more. We may turn the anger back onto ourselves and bottle it up rather than release it.

From the perspective of meditation, the most important aspect of this emotion is to realize that the circuitry for RAGE is wired into us. We can't escape it. But it doesn't mean we have to express it in any specific way. Sometimes it is wise not to vent it in raw form. But it is not wise to pretend it isn't there.

Rage is an extreme emotion. Sometimes we feel something less dramatic, such as anger, irritation, annoyance, or frustration. But if these quieter feelings don't resolve themselves, there may be RAGE underneath. It is helpful to acknowledge it openly to ourselves. When we do so, it is easier to relax into it. The Buddha put his faith in awareness of what we're experiencing inside rather than in a particular outward expression.

There are volumes of research on the dynamics of anger and helpful strategies for working with it wisely. My former therapist used to say that therapy is the art of learning to tolerate feelings. So is meditation. If we can tolerate and allow the feelings to be what they are (or just let them be), they will shift on their own given enough time and clarity. And when we are naturally and openly aware, we know instinctively what to do and what not to do.

FEAR/Anxiety

If I'm sitting in my backyard and I see a raccoon tearing up the bird feeder for the third time this week, I may feel a flash of RAGE. If I see a bear tearing it up, I may feel a flash of FEAR.

FEAR is the third primary emotion. It is the opposite of RAGE in that it motivates us to get away rather than to attack: flight rather than fight.

Yet FEAR is similar to RAGE in that it is usually triggered by a perceived threat. It can send hormones through our system that key us up for action. In humans it often has personal, gender, and cultural conditioning on top of raw biological proclivities. It can fire up the cerebral cortex to generate stories that sometimes help us to sort out what's going on, but often just distract us from the threat or discomfort rather than deeply relieving it.

Libraries are filled with books on fear and techniques for working with it wisely and effectively.

The anatomical wiring is deeply embedded in us, so we can't easily turn these feelings on or off, though we can sometimes numb out or divert the attention we give to them. But even when we try to ignore the feelings, they will have a strong influence that we might not acknowledge.

Paradoxically, if we open awareness to the feelings FEAR triggers, we have more options as to how to respond. By seeing them clearly, it's as if we are taking a step back. We see FEAR/ Anxiety as something we *experience* rather than something we *are*. In that clear seeing we have more time to decide how to respond or not to respond at all.

From a meditative perspective, it's always important to turn *toward* the experience and open up to it so long as we can tolerate it without acting blindly.

Whether we have recurring FEAR or its gentler derivatives, such as worry, anxiety, or edginess, it is helpful to mentally drop the stories and see if there is raw FEAR underneath. Even if we are not tempted to act on that FEAR, it's still helpful to see if it's there in primal form. Then we can turn toward it and relax into this primal emotion.

LUST/Sexual Feelings

For many people, sexual orgasm and its aftermath may come as close to a genuine mystical experience as they'll ever know. The sense of being a separate self can melt into the background as consciousness expands into wellbeing, contentment, and equanimity. It's not surprising that this is one of the primordial affective emotions.

However, Panksepp's term for it — "LUST" — can be misleading. In the dictionary, the word "sexual" means "relating to, or associated with sex," while "lust" means "unusually intense or unbridled sexual desire" or, more generally, craving for anything.

The fourth affective emotion of LUST (capitalized) might be better described as "sexual feeling." However, that phrase can include sexual fantasies, romantic stories, plans, and other thoughts that have considerable cortical involvement. The affective emotions are precognitive mid and lower brain functions.

The phrase "precognitive mid and lower brain sexual feeling" is long and awkward. Perhaps this is why Panksepp used "LUST" and signaled that his capitalized terms do not always align with their common usage or dictionary definitions. In other words, LUST does not mean "lust." It means "precognitive sexual feelings."

Precognitive sexual feelings have obvious evolutionary importance: without them the species dies out. So, they can be powerful motivators and find wide varieties of expression. They can also strengthen interpersonal bonds, resulting in more than one adult providing care for young ones, for example.

Sexual feelings can also distort and disrupt social bonds in individuals and communities. So it's not surprising that there are taboos about when, how, and with whom to express them, as well as attempts to squelch them all together.

From a meditative perspective, awareness of the reality of our inner experience is part of the road to freedom. Sexual feelings are natural, wired in, and change over time. Finding clear, peaceful, kind, genuine, and satisfying ways to be with sexual energy is always helpful.

CARE/Nurturing

CARE is more altruistic than LUST. Mammals and birds are so helpless at birth that they would not survive without care from others. These emotions are especially strong toward young ones, though the emotions can spread out to focus on peers and elders and even the young of other species. A quiet joy can emerge from satisfying, caring exchanges.

CARE, the fifth affective emotion, is so important that it is wired into children, even though the evolutionary imperative is less germane until they are older.

When she was eighteen months old, our granddaughter had a few dolls. She often spread out a tiny doll blanket on the rug, placed a doll on the blanket, wrapped it up, held it against her chest, and patted it on the back as she smiled. After a few moments, she dropped the doll on its head and crawled off to do something else.

Her expression of CARE lacked refinement — after all she was not even two years old. What was remarkable was that the affective emotion was obvious even at such a young age.

In meditation it is helpful to savor CARING feelings when they arise. And as with all emotions, it helps to look beyond the stories to what we actually sense in the moment.

CONNECTION/Panic and Grief

CONNECTION is the urge to reach out to others, particularly when we are in need of support. In some ways it is the inverse of CARE — it's the urge to connect with someone for our own sake rather than for theirs. And it's distinct enough to have its own neural wiring cluster. It's the sixth affective emotion.

Without this instinct we would be less likely to survive and pass our genes along. So, when support is not forthcoming, panic arises in the short run and grief in the long run. Panic and grief are more obvious expressions of this primary emotion, but the urge for CONNECTION is its deeper source and the name I favor. Here's a nuanced example:

My friend's four-year-old daughter, Janie, asked her dad, "How long do we go on for?"

"I don't know," her dad said. After a pause he added, "My grandfather died in his sixties. His father died when he was in his late nineties."

Janie was quiet for a few moments. Then she asked, "Am I going to die?"

"Yes," her dad said softly, "but probably not for a long time."

Janie's lip began to quiver. Her eyes moistened. "I don't want to die. I'll miss you and mommy."

Her dad could have said, "When you die, you won't miss anybody because you won't be here." But he had the good sense to skip logic and respond from a deeper place. He put his arm around her and said, "I love you so much." Janie snuggled in and gradually settled down.

Notice three emotions: panic, sadness, and the urge to connect.

Sometimes these emotions can be more dramatic. Early in his career, Jaak Panksepp noted how baby rats emitted distinctive, high-pitched squeals when separated from their mothers. They sounded terrified.[6]

A human infant who is happy, dry, and well-fed but left alone for too long will start to cry. Picking her up and talking softly is often enough comfort so that the crying subsides. It's easy to see similar dynamics in other mammals and birds.

At times in his career, Panksepp called this primary affective emotion PANIC with grief as a relevant expression. Other times he called it SADNESS with panic as a relevant

---

[6] Panksepp and Biven, *The Archaeology of Mind,* Kindle version, p. 315.

expression. Sadness and panic are part of this emotion and either or both can arise. I was struck by this relationship between panic and sadness. Once Panksepp's writing pointed it out to me, it made sense intuitively.

My therapist once noted that I seemed to be in a frozen startle underneath. I often noticed this as fretfulness that I could trace to my early years. I also knew it was easy for me to feel lonely, which also seemed left over from my childhood.

When fretfulness or loneliness arise in meditation, I often Six-R them or simply turn toward and relax into them. They subside — but sometimes only for a while. Sometimes they keep returning in other ways.

On the other hand, if I feel beneath the fretfulness or sadness, I can often sense a quiet urge to be with others. If I relax into that feeling, it often spreads out and quiets as my mind-heart settles into a deep peace that can then follow me through the day.

So, when I think of the various components of this affect, CONNECTION seems to be the deepest. Panic, fretfulness, sadness, and grief are signals that come up when it is not fulfilled. However, to be fully open and relaxed with the urge itself — whether it's fulfilled or not — is often enough for me to drift toward nirodha — the cessation of perception, feeling, and consciousness.

In traditional Buddhist terminology, unfulfilled CONNECTION is a cause and condition of panic, sadness, and grief. When CONNECTION is there, panic and grief do not arise. So I have found it more helpful to think of this emotion as CONNECTION.

Note: The panic may be reminiscent of FEAR. But with closer examination, it is quite different. FEAR is triggered by the presence of a predator or other threat. Panic is the loss of CONNECTION and is triggered by the absence of a nurturer or other support. Furthermore, they light up different areas of the lower brain. FEAR centers in the central amygdala while panic centers in the dorsal thalamus, basal forebrain nuclei, and subcallosal anterior cingulate.

Another place where CONNECTION may be seen is inner talk. A long time ago I noticed that my inner thinking was often in the form of explanations. Sometimes I was mentally talking to a specific person. Other times there was no specific person in my mind, but there was a general sense of talking to someone. The urge to CONNECT was an element of my inner chatter.

If I turned toward and relaxed into the chatter, it often subsided for a while, only to pop up again in a different thought or story. But sometimes I noticed an urge for CONNECTION. This urge was a building block out of which the inner chatter arose. It might be in the form of subtle (or not so subtle) loneliness or fretfulness. If, without trying to get rid of the lonesome feelings or fretful thinking, I relaxed into them, the inner conversation tended to fade away for much longer because it had grown out of those feeling.

Another aspect of CONNECTION is imaginary friends. Some children have imaginary playmates. They talk about them as if they were real, though most know they aren't.

Recently I realized that I, too, have imaginary friends — a lot of them. When I'm walking in the woods, lying awake in bed, or sitting in meditation I may have spontaneous silent conversations with them. I refer to this simply as "thinking," but when I look at the flow of thoughts, they sound more like a dialogue with an imaginary friend.

I know they aren't real, though many of them bear a close resemblance to people I know — usually people with whom I have some tension at that moment. At other times they are vaguely generic.

As I write these words, it's as if I'm talking to a generic reader, how they (or you) might respond, and how I might reply. Perhaps most, if not all, of the thoughts in my head are embedded in some kind of inner discussion. After all, the nature of speech is communication.

I don't like to think of myself as crazy enough to talk with someone who isn't here. But I do so silently all the time. Perhaps it's just the nature of us humans that speech is spoken thought and thought is silent speaking. Our instincts for CONNECTION often take the shape of dialogue.

PLAY/Joy and Lovable Oddity

Our grandson was sitting on a swing seat suspended from a maple tree by two 15-foot ropes. He continued his countdown: "...four-three-two-one-blast off." Taking my cue, I swung him back and forth, higher and higher. Then he exclaimed, "We're in outer space!" On this particular afternoon he imagined us landing in Australia to see the kangaroos before blasting off to Africa and then to Mexico to visit the monkeys.

Before leaving "Mexico," he began messing around with a plastic lawn chair lying on its side near the swing. As he lifted it, he swung one leg up over the arm of the chair and used the other leg to push off away from the ground. The chair righted itself with him still on the chair's arm. He laughed with delight and tried it again. This time he tumbled to the ground and laughed. And I laughed with him. After fooling around with the chair for a while, he pulled it over to the swing and tried to crawl from the chair to the swing without touching the ground.

When it worked, he laughed. When he tumbled to the ground, he laughed.

"Rocket ship" and "Tumble-the-chair" were two different kinds of play. Rocket ship used speech, stories, and imagination. If he'd been wearing a brain monitor, we'd have seen a lot of activity in the neocortex from his language and stories. This kind of play includes strategy games such as checkers, chess, cards, and board games.

Tumble-the-chair used very little language or stories. A brain monitor would have shown the subcortical circuitry for what Jaak Panksepp called PLAY, the seventh primary affective emotion. This kind of PLAY is primarily rough-and-tumble horsing around, or just plain goofiness. It includes minimal use of speech or language.

When studying PLAY, Panksepp sometimes put two children in a room that was empty except for a mat. He invited them to "play and have fun." Often, they ran around, chased each other, pushed each other, and so on.

From an adult perspective, these activities can help children learn physical mastery, social skills, and more. But from the kids' perspective, their activities were not goal directed. And they were always accompanied by laughter no matter what the outcome.

This non-goal-directed free-form PLAY is wired into us. Children need a certain amount of PLAY to grow into happy, socially sensitive adults. Without it they are statistically more likely to become delinquent, criminal, or depressed as adults.

The most important age for PLAY may be the "terrible twos," when unstructured activity can be confused with ADHD (attention deficit hyperactivity disorder). But some subcortical play can last into human adulthood. In some animals, it disappears as they grow up. But in all mammals and birds, a certain amount of PLAY in the early years helps them develop into happy, socially sensitive adults. The brain needs PLAY to learn how to interact and enjoy others without bullying or other distortions.

Research has also revealed that some of the areas that light up in primary affective PLAY also light up while we are dreaming. Of course, dream sleep is accompanied by atonia, in which the large muscles remain relaxed though smaller muscles that control eyes, fingers, lips, and more may remain active.

The relationship between PLAY and dreaming is provocative and intriguing. Compared to normal waking consciousness, both playing and dreaming are less constrained by the laws of physics and are shaped more by emotion, whim, and unconscious urges.

PLAY has important implications for meditation as well as for our daily lives. When my kids were growing up, I used to call PLAY "fadoodling." My grandson's chair tumbling was fadoodling because he enjoyed it and laughed no matter what the outcome. It was not goal directed.

As an adult, I sometimes call PLAY "puttering" — something I do more because I enjoy it rather than because I think I have to accomplish anything tangible.

Athletes may call it "being in the zone." While it may aid high performance, when an athlete or a chess master is "in the zone," they enjoy their frame of mind-heart in the moment as much as or more than when they win the game.

In a similar way, PLAY in meditation is not a special practice or technique so much as simple joy in whatever we are doing or not doing. We cannot attain it — there is nothing to be gained. But we can attune to it, because it's always here.

It's a paradox: we can't *attain* higher jhānas, nirodha, or nibbāna. The attempt to *get there* will make it ultimately impossible. We can only *be there*. We may spontaneously drop into it by just being *here*. But if we try to get *there*, it won't work.

So, in formal meditation, if we let the mind do what it wants and simply see where it lands, this does not guarantee we will "get there." But without this attitude, we can never be fully there. Or here.

In meditation PLAY is an attitude to be felt, not a task to be accomplished. A relaxed, playful mind is more sensitive and perceptive than one that tries too hard. If we take meditation or ourselves too seriously, we may benefit by practicing goofiness off the cushion and relaxed pleasure on the cushion.

We'll come back to this when we talk about homeostasis and finding healthy balances in life. For now, it's helpful to remember to take joy in life's oddities. Carmen Bernos de Gasztold captured this spirit in his "Prayer of the Elephant"[7]:

Dear God,
it is I, the elephant,
Your creature,
who is talking to You.
I am so embarrassed by my great self,
and truly it is not my fault
if I spoil Your jungle a little with my big feet.
Let me be careful and behave wisely,
always keeping my dignity and poise.
Give me such philosophic thoughts

---

[7] *Prayers from the Ark* (Penguin Books, 1976).

that I can rejoice everywhere I go
in the lovable oddity of things.
Amen

Regardless of what emotions arise, they come out of the body. So it is often helpful to see if you sense something more in one part of the body than in another. If so, you can let go of any labels and let awareness settle into the center of the actual sensation. This lets you be with it on its own terms rather than through a mental label. Sometimes that is enough to allow it to relax and unwind on its own.

No Escape

Since these seven affective emotions are wired into us, we are not to blame for them and we cannot escape them completely. They can be modified, attenuated, exaggerated, and otherwise shaped by the neocortex through experience. They can be contained or expressed in lots of different ways. But they cannot be avoided entirely. And if we try to ignore them, they will find subconscious expressions. Suppressed anger might show up as a sharp edge in our voice. Ignored fear may show up as a bit of hypervigilance. And so forth.

On the other hand, if we acknowledge and explore them, we can find wise and generous ways to be with them. They may guide our feelings, but with increasing awareness, we can use them wisely and generously.

In the next two chapters, we'll look at ways of doing just that. We'll look at them through the lens of Buddhist practice and look at Buddhist practice through the lens of affective emotions. Chapters 3 and 4 offer the Buddhist view of spaciousness and Chapter 5 lays out the specifics of Buddhist meditation and how to cultivate this broad view.

Summary

Table 1: Summary of the Affective Emotions, giving the essence of their original purpose.

Primary Emotion	Secondary Emotions	Notes	Page Ref
SEEKING	Expectancy	Explore for resources (dopamine)	pp. 16-18
RAGE	Anger	Defend and compete for resources	pp. 18-20
FEAR	Anxiety	Escape bodily damage	pp. 20-21
LUST	Sexual Feelings	Find mates, intimacy, reproducing, pleasure	p. 21
CARE	Nurturing	Care for offspring	pp. 21-23
CONNEC-TION	Panic and Grief	Distress signals help maintain social bonds, especially for the young	pp. 23-27
PLAY	Joy	Social bonding and learning social limits	pp. 27-31

Consciousness

A final word on affective emotions and consciousness…

While the primordial affective emotions are *among* the sources of consciousness, they are not the *only* source. They are not by themselves *the* determinant of consciousness or unconsciousness. The neuroscientific evidence suggests a delicate interdependent web of areas of the brain that together give rise to consciousness and a sense of self. These areas include the affective emotions along with the hypothalamus, periaqueductal gray, superior colliculi, parabrachial nucleus, area postrema, nucleus tractus solitarius, posteromedial cortex (PMC), and more. No single site works alone or has ultimate control. However, I'd like to emphasize what I said at the beginning of this chapter:

> Of all these structures, the affective emotions are the easiest to identify in our direct, subjective experience. I and many of my students can attest to that.
>
> Of all the factors relevant to consciousness, primordial emotions are uniquely accessible through introspection. Working wisely with them helps us walk the path laid out by the Buddha. Relaxing them moves us along the Buddha's map toward nirodha (cessation of consciousness) and even nibbāna (extinction of consciousness), accompanied by deep awakening.

3

Relax and Expand: Spaciousness and the Negativity Bias

Suppose a person dropped a lump of salt into a small bowl of water. Would that water become salty and undrinkable?
Yes, sir.
Why is that?
Because there is only a little water in the bowl.
Suppose a person dropped a lump of salt into the Ganges River. Would the Ganges become salty and undrinkable?
No, sir.
Why is that?
Because the Ganges is vast.

— the Buddha
Lonaphala Sutta ("The Lump of Salt")
Anguttara Nikāya 3.99

The Buddha was unusual in insisting that suffering is a part of life in this world. Life has its lumps of salt. Compared to other spiritual traditions, this may sound pessimistic. But before we diagnose him with a mood disorder, it behooves us to look closely at what he actually said. He never said life *is* a bummer.

He only said life <u>*has*</u> bummers. Have you never felt let down, sad, or disappointed? Do you know anyone who has never gone through hard times?

I didn't think so.

In Buddhism there is no "fake it 'til you make it." True spirituality is not possible unless it is rooted in a clear-eyed, open-hearted, uncompromising view of life as it is — not what we want, prefer, fear, or yearn for, but how it really is. This is not where the Buddha *ended up*. This is where he *began*: life has its lumps of salt.

When life becomes salty or undrinkable, our natural reflex is to wince, turn away, or contract as if we could push the salt out of our system. Self-protection is wired into us. We can't help it if we sometimes feel sad or upset and want some distance.

The Buddha said in effect, "Let's not waste energy on the fantasy that life doesn't have bitter moments. We can't alter what is real or how we feel about it. However, if we don't fight reality, we have more energy to respond creatively to what is before us."

This subtle, aikido-like move recognizes that we have little choice about what happens around us or arises unbidden within us, but we have some freedom as to how we engage it. This is a counterintuitive secret: it is helpful to expand and make our inner space bigger.

The difference between depression and enlightenment is the difference between contracting and expanding, between shrinking and opening up, between being a small bowl of water and being the Ganges River. It doesn't get rid of the salt. But if we're as big as the Ganges, we may not notice it.

I know, today the Ganges is a sewer in many places. But in the Buddha's day it was clear, clean, vast, and flowed gently for miles until it merged with the ocean. How do we expand our container so that our mind-heart is like the Ganges the Buddha knew: serene, spacious, wise, and heartful?

With presence and compassion we can influence how we relate to life. So, let's use that influence not to shrink into existential dread but to spread out beyond the boundaries of selfdom and merge with all of life, out of which we emerged. When we do this, the lump of salt is no big deal. It's a small thing. And it doesn't separate us from wisdom, contentment, serenity, and a sense of belonging.

The Negativity Bias

In the next chapter we'll explore the nitty-gritty details of the meditation practice the Buddha recommended. But before doing that, let's get a feel for where it is heading.

To make this less theoretical, let's look at a specific reflex that encourages us to shrink rather than expand, and then let us consider how to gracefully turn that around.

This reflex is often called the "negativity bias." It's so pervasive that it seems like it's part of our neural anatomy. And it can distort our thinking. However, unlike the affective emotions, we can't find wiring for it in the brain. Some dispute its existence. But its effects are real and measurable.

Here's an example of the negativity bias: Imagine receiving a job review that describes your performance as

Diligent
Knowledgeable
Cooperative
Not punctual
Sincere

A month later, the item you're most likely to remember is "not punctual." It sticks with you. Scientists have found that with jobs, books, vacations, movies, and so on, the ratio is about 3:1 — it takes about three positives to counterbalance one negative. In evaluating people and social situations, the ratio is about 5:1.

This is the negativity bias.

The phenomenon is real. There is a lot of scientific research documenting how it works and its implications. And there is a seemingly obvious evolutionary explanation.

Imagine you are walking through a primordial forest and see a wolf coming toward you and, at the same time, you see an enticing piece of fruit hanging on a nearby tree. If you are more sensitive to the negatives than the positives, you deal with the wolf first: fight or flight. If you get away without getting killed, you come back for the fruit later.

If you are more sensitive to positives than to negatives, you go for the fruit first and ignore the wolf. In this case, you're more likely to be eaten by the predator or otherwise have your genes removed from the gene pool.

Evolution is not about our wellbeing or objectivity. It's about staying alive long enough to breed. We can breed if we're unhappy or deluded. But we can't breed if we're dead. So, natural selection favors a bit of paranoia.

When I first encountered this thought experiment, as cogent seemed, it left me uneasy. It was based on armchair philosophy rather than hard data. Careful studies of the brain pinpoint specific areas responsible for each affective emotion. But, as noted, the negativity bias does not map explicitly to any brain structure. It may be an artifact of the SEEKING affective emotion. As you may remember (Chapter 2), SEEKING responds to novelty. When something new or mysterious shows up, a little dopamine is injected into the brain to perk us up, and our attention is drawn to the surprise: "What's that?"

There are SEEKING circuits that draw our awareness to both pleasant and unpleasant events. While it may seem like the negatives are stronger, carefully controlled studies suggest the draw is equal in both directions. In fact, the attracting circuits outnumber the aversive circuits in most mammals, including humans.

These positive biases arose early in evolution and suggest that they are more basic to the overall neurology. Large predatory reptiles dominated the land when the first mammals appeared. It would have been to the mammals' advantage to keep a low profile. They were small — the size of modern shrews, rats, and squirrels — and probably nocturnal. Their eating habits did not draw undue attention. They were foragers who probably felt some pleasure grazing or quietly sniffing through dead trees for insects or through dirt for roots and bulbs.

Therefore today, the negativity bias may be due to there being more pleasant than unpleasant experiences around us. In other words, this bias may not be inherent to the brain as was once thought. Rather it is more likely to be the result of negative experiences being more noticeable today because they are less frequent. They stand out in our minds due to their novelty.[8]

The meditation teacher Jack Kornfield frames it from a slightly different point of view:

---

[8] Thanks to Richard Maddock, MD, of the University of California Davis School of Medicine, in Sacramento, California, for helping me sort out the finer points.

> *Anyone can see that if grasping and aversion were with us all day and night without ceasing, who could ever stand them? Under that condition, living things would either die or become insane. Instead, we survive because there are natural periods of coolness, of wholeness, and ease. In fact, they last longer than the fires of our grasping and fear. It is this that sustains us. We have periods of rest making us refreshed, alive, well.*[9]

A Wider View

In other words, to understand the negativity bias, we may need to expand our frame of reference to include a diverse range of biological, personal, social, and cultural contexts. We need to be less like a bowl and more like a river.

Let's look again at surprise and threat in the earlier examples.

In the job evaluation, if others had commented on your lateness and you were well aware of it yourself, then "not punctual" would not have been a surprise. It would not have been a big deal. And if you had been worried about your job because you didn't feel you knew enough, being called "knowledgeable" would have been a surprise. It would stand out more clearly in your mind over the following months.

In this larger context, the negativity bias is less important; surprise and threat are more salient.

Here's another example of how context matters. As I write these words, I am excited about the heavy rain outside. I've lived in the semi-arid Central Valley of Northern California for about twenty years. In past decades, it hardly rained at all in the spring and summer but rained a lot in the late fall and winter. The natives complained about how gloomy the rain

---

[9] *After the Ecstasy, the Laundry* (2001, Bantam Books, 2001).

was. When I first moved here from New England, I told them, "Gloomy? You have no idea what bad weather is."

However, after a few years of sunny springs and summers, I, too, found the rain gloomy too — a definite negative bias.

In the last few years, the winter rains have dried up. I worry about climate change, the loss of water to the region, the possibility that this land may be less livable in the near future.

In this context, I'm happy to have the rain. I'm sure I'll remember it more not because it's a negative but because it is unusual now. And it definitely feels pleasant.

When we consider the larger context, arousal seems to be the most potent variable that affects our attention. And threat, by definition, arouses us. Novelty, arousal, and threat may account for the negativity bias more than negative biological wiring.

On the other side of the equation, "inspiration" might be a word applied to positives. Inspiration and threat have opposite vectors and pull us in opposite directions. And because both are relatively rare, they stand out.

Social Implications

Placing the negativity bias in a wider context has implications for humanity in today's world. Our wired-in instincts emerged over hundreds of thousands of years when we lived in tribes and small groups. We are not well suited to cope with the power of modern technology nor the speed and spread of modern communications because our instincts are from a world utterly different in essential ways from our current techno-info culture.

Cell phones, the Internet, and social media don't allow for the depth of empathy that arises spontaneously when we know people's histories and can see them, hear them, hug them, and look into their eyes. Today we interact with and depend upon more people without knowing them than we did when we lived in clans and tribes and knew fewer people but knew them well. We are ill-equipped biologically to handle the effects of information technology and social media algorithms.

Social media companies want to know their users' preferences. Rather than converse with thousands of people, their software adds up how often a certain person clicks a particular item on a Web page. Engineers figure the more clicking, the higher the interest. From a certain perspective, that seems innocuous enough. Advertisers and social media platforms can then send different users different information depending on the users' preferences.

However, when we factor in how arousal and threat can engender a negativity bias in us, we end up having our complaints and grievances echoed back to us three to five times more than our wisdom and equanimity. We are soon awash in anger and stress. And our collective equanimity, wisdom, and even civility get swamped.

Like every other human quality, the degree to which we are affected by arousal and stress varies from person to person. Those who have a stronger negativity bias tend to be more interested in safety: punishing criminals, promoting military strength, supporting strong police and large corporations to protect us, etc. They gravitate toward conservative causes. Those with a weaker negativity bias have more interest in wellbeing: helping the unfortunate, health care, education, the environment, etc. They gravitate toward liberal and progressive causes.

Politicians of all stripes know that although people say they prefer positive advertising and messages, in reality they show up and vote more when motivated by what they are against than by what they are for. We can see the effects of this in the degeneration of the public discourse into bickering and sanctimonious critiques. There are fewer areas of agreement between rival political parties.

Some of the greatest problems facing us today — ecological collapse, political polarization, and economic stratification — are exacerbated by a human species whose social instincts are better suited to small towns and clans than to urban centers with millions of people gazing at their TVs and cell phones.

Enlarging the Container

A more in-depth exploration of ecology, mass media, political polarization, and the like is beyond the scope of this book. I'm more interested in consciousness and how we can deepen our wisdom, compassion, and wellbeing without shutting out the world or getting too deeply entangled in it. How can we find peace within and peace with all of our neighbors near and far? And these days, our inner consciousness and how we get along with each other seem to be more and more intimately tied together.

The good news is that the negativity bias is not wired into us. If we look deeply and skillfully inside, we are not doomed to getting mired in ancient tarpits of ill will. Inspiration can grab our attention as effectively as threats. They have equal strength, though opposite vectors.

The Buddha lived in a technologically simpler time. But the brain has not evolved significantly since he walked along the Ganges River. He deeply understood the human mind. That wisdom is still relevant today.

His image of the lump of salt in the Ganges suggests we hold our difficulties clearly but lightly. Holding tight hurts in and of itself. And when we hurt, this signals the brain that there is a problem. It tends to contract into emergency mode. Since thinking is one of our survival tools, the brain starts thinking more rapidly and less wisely.

Therefore, rather than contract, the Buddha suggests that we expand our container (our field of consciousness) so that we can see a larger and longer context. And at the same time we relax so that the mind-heart becomes less obsessive and fixated and more creative and flexible.

Reverse Paranoia

Another metaphor for this insight is "reverse paranoia." Paranoia is thinking the universe is out to get me or at least trying to exclude me. Reverse paranoia is imagining that the universe is out to lift me up or at least make sure I'm included. Since the universe is not a person but an impersonal web, I might say that the universe is just what it is and does what it does without paying attention to me at all. Since I arose out of the natural world, I have a place here in the interdependence of things.

Radical Acceptance

Radical acceptance takes this one step further.

In my early years of meditation, I felt it was important to see clearly and openly exactly how things were. It wasn't that the universe was needy or wanted my approval so that it could feel better. Rather, the more clearly and heartfully I could see my situation, the more likely I'd see a course through a difficult circumstance.

What was radical about this acceptance was that, in truth, sometimes I didn't like my situation. It didn't help to pretend I liked something I actually felt aversion toward. Yet it did help me when I accepted my dislike without struggling. It helped me to accept my lack of acceptance and to relax into all of it.

The acceptance of dislike and inner whininess allowed those feelings to be what they were. By not fighting with inner moods, my inner view became easier and more expansive, even if there was a taste of bitterness. But it became a little saltiness rather than a big deal.

All I had to do was to see reality without fighting it. Then my awareness became less like a small bowl of water and more like an impersonal ocean. In that expansive view there was wisdom and clarity.[10]

Don't Fight Reality

Radical acceptance boils down to three words: "Don't fight reality." It takes a fraction of a moment for sensory signals to be transmitted to the brain and processed. What we experience as "this moment" is already a fraction of a second into the past. To reject "this moment" is to fight with the past. Good luck with that! As Lily Tomlin put it, "Forgiveness is giving up all hope of having a better past."

The only sane attitude is to accept reality as it is and to expand and relax at the same time. These are the causes and conditions that encourage wisdom, kindness, and courage to rise in future moments.

---

[10] Tara Brach apparently came to a similar insight in her life. Her book by this name, *Radical Acceptance* (Bantam Books, 2003), is a well-written exploration of the topic from many angles.

Excitement Without Oxygen — Don't Push So Hard

To take this even further, my former therapist once described anxiety as excitement without oxygen. If we relax into our anxiousness and let our breathing go deeper, anxiety may be less constrained; it can spread out and feel more like excitement.

In my book *Buddha's Map,* I briefly describe meditating in Thailand with Ajahn Tong. At that time, he worked directly with very few Westerners. His initial instructions to me were, "Work hard and diligently." I told him my teachers in America told me I used too much effort and should relax in order to stay balanced.

He said, "No. 'Right effort' means using strong determination to stay mindful and follow the instructions."

I was not sure that was right for me. But he was a revered Thai master and I had come all the way around the world to train with him. It seemed wise to put my doubt aside and follow his instructions while I was there. Later on I could evaluate my experience. I went back to my *kuti* and tried my best to follow his advice.

In my next interview, I told him what I had been doing. As I spoke, his eyes grew wider and wider. Then he said, "Take a walk. Relax. Buy some ice cream. You're pushing too hard."

In a flash I got it. He mostly taught Thai and other Southeast Asians. I found most Thai to be sweet, gentle, kind, and fun-loving. I couldn't imagine them meditating as hard as I was. He had been talking to me in the same way he spoke to his Thai students. From then on, whenever he gave me instructions, I listened as if I had a kind, mellow, Thai temperament. Then I felt more like the Ganges and less like a cup of water.

Often I found that my anxiety was "excitement without oxygen." Giving it more space left me feeling more spacious. With this, Ajahn Tong's instructions worked much better.

Luminous Mind

Another way to describe a vast Ganges-like awareness is to notice the spaciousness, clarity, and natural luminosity of the mind-heart that are already with us. They never leave. However, they are very quiet. It's easy for them to get covered over or for us to simply not notice.

In the next chapter we'll look at some of the practices the Buddha taught to help us notice the quiet, luminous mind that often hides in plain sight. And we'll look at the nitty-gritty aspects of simple and direct daily meditation practice.

Relaxing and Expanding

In the *Lonaphala Sutta* quoted earlier, the Buddha encourages us to allow awareness to relax and expand so that it notices the field of awareness rather than just the objects in it. We notice the vastness of the Ganges that holds the tiny lump of salt. If we're walking through a meadow, rather than just noticing the flowers, trees, butterflies, and birds we also take in the loveliness of the meadow itself that holds all that flora and fauna. If we're gazing at the sky on a clear night, we let our awareness relax and expand to take in more than the stars. We open to the vastness of the space between the stars. Without that space there would be no stars or planets or anything. Nothing would exist.

Similarly, the Buddha encouraged us to let awareness relax and expand beyond the content of the mind and notice the field of awareness that holds that content.

The objects are things. The field is not a thing — it is no-thing or nothing. It is empty space within which flowers, birds, stars, people, thoughts, and feelings can arise and vanish.

As awareness shifts from things to awareness itself, it is easier for things to arise and vanish without us identifying with them. That is freedom.

The other practices that we explored in this chapter — enlarging the container, reverse paranoia, radical acceptance, excitement without oxygen, and luminous mind — are just variations on the theme of mitigating suffering by shifting attention from the salt to the Ganges, from the stars to space, from the objects in the mind to awareness itself, and yes, from the self as an object to the awareness that sees the sense of self arise and fade.

None of these practices are about getting rid of difficulties. They are about making room for suffering with such generosity of spirit that the salt dissolves in the expansiveness. We're not trying to defeat pain. We're trying to learn how to be with it openheartedly enough that it ceases to be a problem.

Without this attitude, the Buddha's meditation practice ultimately won't work. Rather than trying to segregate experience into good and bad, happiness and pain, liking and disliking, we use them all to open up to all of life.

4

Spectrum of Awareness

The last chapter explored relaxation and expansion. This chapter explores the Spectrum of Awareness as a practical tool for integrating relaxation and expansion into our meditation practices. Table 2 offers a conceptual overview.

Table 2: Spectrum of Awareness

Phase	Examples
1. Content	Plans, stories, ideas, problems, friends, foes
2. Processes	Thinking, worrying, storytelling, figuring, planning, arguing, daydreaming
3. Qualities of awareness	Clear, foggy, agitated, calm, fast, sluggish, sticky, spacious, open, tight
4. Field of Awareness	Noticing awareness apart from its content, process, qualities, or textures
5. Nothingness	Emptiness, "winking out," nirodha, nibbāna

Actually, rather than a table of separate boxes, the Spectrum might be better illustrated by a gradient in which each phase blends with its neighbor:

Content	Process	Qualities	Awareness	Nothing

Like most of Buddhism, the Spectrum of Awareness is a phenomenology. It's not a philosophical or intellectual construct. And it's certainly not metaphysics or theology. It's a description of direct experience — phenomena — rather than ideas about experience.

The Buddha realized that if we can know what we are experiencing clearly enough and relax about it, that is the beginning of the end of suffering. So, he advocated awareness of phenomena as they are rather than explanations of what they represent philosophically.

Content

The first phase of the Spectrum of Awareness is content. The evolutionary function of awareness is to see the content of experience and develop a map of what's out there: bird, tree, rock, river, etc. Some objects have more charge: a guy with a spear, a dog with its teeth bared. The greater the charge, the more the mind shrink-wraps around the object(s).

Processes

As the mind-heart relaxes and expands, we may begin to notice the second phase of the Spectrum: the processes out of which the objects arise. We notice the thinking, feeling, daydreaming, and other processes the mind is engaged in doing rather than focusing only on the *contents* of thinking, feeling, daydreaming, and so forth.

Like the contents, the processes can also be light (musing, wondering, fantasizing) or more energized (complaining, worrying, arguing, defending). But as the mind relaxes and expands, the contents drift into the background and the processes become clearer.

Qualities

As we become more aware of the processes, we may start to notice the qualities of awareness that give rise to the processes. Awareness can be light, serene, peaceful, or easygoing. Or its qualities may be more energetic: anger, fear, urgency, excitement, obsessiveness.

As we notice the qualities, the mind-heart naturally relaxes and expands. And it works the other way around as well: as the mind-heart relaxes and expands, we become more aware of the subtle qualities of awareness.

Field of Awareness

As the qualities become more apparent, we may start to notice the field of awareness itself. We may notice the effects of being aware. At the end of the last chapter I described this as analogous to taking in the field of an entire meadow rather than just zeroing in on the plants and animals in it. Or looking into a moonless night and sensing the empty space between the star rather than just the celestial objects. On a smaller scale it is liking meeting a new person and being struck by their overall presence rather than just their freckles or socks; or taking in the ambience of a crowd of people rather than just a few individuals.

We also notice the field of awareness any time we take in the quality of our awareness itself rather than just the objects we see.

Nothingness

If we are aware of awareness and continue to relax and expand, we may notice the nothingness out of which phenomena and awareness arise. In meditation, these first manifest as short blank spots in our attention. We may wonder if we had drifted off to sleep for a moment.

However, when we doze and come back, the mind is often a little dense or foggy. But as the mind-heart relaxes and expands, there may be blank spots followed by clear awareness (as alluded to in the subtitle of this book). In this case, it is less likely that we actually fell asleep and more likely that the mind became so relaxed that awareness itself stopped functioning for a moment. The Buddha called these blank spots "nirodha" — the cessation of perception, feeling, and consciousness.

When cessation is deep enough, the mind-heart that returns is not exactly like the one we once knew. The objects, concepts, and sense of self that once predominated have receded far into the background of irrelevance. This is a sign of nibbāna — a topic for another time.

From the perspective of the awareness, we have relaxed and expanded from one end of the Spectrum to the other. The Buddha called this end "the extinction of suffering."

Upside Down

I presented these phases starting with the one we are mostly likely to be aware of first: the content. As awareness quiets, it becomes easier to see the *processes that generated that content*. As the mind quiets some more, we may see the *qualities that generated the processes*. And so on through awareness itself and the nothingness out of which awareness arises.

Notice that philosophically we could have turned the sequence on its head and started with the formlessness out of which awareness itself emerges, and in turn out of which qualities, processes, and content emerge. We could reasonably present the opposite sequence.

And we could have presented the Spectrum without any sequence. The term *paṭiccasamuppāda* is usually translated as "dependent origination" which suggests a linear series where each phase is the origin the next. But the term more accurately translates as "dependent co-arising." The spectrum emerges whole cloth, as it were. Thich Nhat Hanh calls this "interbeing." Rather than a line of falling dominos, a better image is a web where everything is connected to everything else in a mind-boggling complexity.

But we don't have to pick winners and losers in this debate. As I indicated earlier, the Buddha was most interested in a practical resolution of suffering. For that purpose, awareness of the phenomena is enough. The present moment contains everything we need to be free if we can see it clearly and deeply enough.

Meanwhile, as emerging awareness of the present deepens, don't be surprised if some of our ideas about how things work get thrown overboard.

Implications for Meditation

To take the Spectrum of Awareness into meditation, the general idea is to gradually shift our attention from the contents of awareness across the Spectrum. This shift is often easier and more graceful when done in small, natural movements from content, to process, to qualities of awareness, to awareness itself, to the nothingness out of which awareness arises.

The most obvious difference between various styles of meditation is the "home base" that is recommended to help settle the practice. Often it's called the "object of meditation." This side of enlightenment we can count on the mind wandering — sometimes a lot. When we notice this, the instructions are to return our attention to this homebase.

Tension is a cause and condition that encourages the mind to wander more. The art is to return to home base without being critical of ourselves or tightening up in other ways. Instead, we relax and expand as we come back to the home base.

My favorite practice for doing this is embedded in the Buddha's teaching of the Four Noble Truths. A slightly more elaborate version, called the Six Rs, was developed by Bhante Vimalaraṁsi and is particularly helpful when the mind is very jumbled.

I've written about these practices in *Buddha's Map* and subsequent books.[11] However, I review the most relevant parts in Chapters 5 and 6 and Appendix A of this book.

Regardless of what strategies we use to get the mind-heart back on the path, if it includes relaxing and expanding, it will tend to move the mind along the Spectrum of Awareness.

In the remainder of this chapter I want to explore our choice of objects for that home base and how to integrate that choice with the Spectrum of Awareness. This makes

---

[11] *Buddha's Map* (2013), *Meditator's Field Guide* (2017), *Befriending the Mind* (2019), and *Resting in the Waves* (2020).

meditation more dynamic and responsive and helps wisdom and compassion arise more easily.

To see this, let's look at some of the objects that are used as a home base — the breath, mettā, and objectless awareness — as well as how to make the practice more flexible and responsive to our experience.

The Breath

The breath is a widely used home base. The most obvious aspect of the breath is its content (phase 1 of the Spectrum): the actual sensations in the chest or tip of the nose.

If we notice these, it is easy and natural to open up a little further on the Spectrum to the *process* of breathing (phase 2): the rising and falling of the diaphragm, chest, or the subtle movements throughout the body.

If we do this, it is easier to notice the *qualities* of the breath (phase 3). It may feel light, heavy, gentle, tense, ragged, etc.

If we notice the qualities, it is easier to notice the *subtle effects of being aware* (phase 4) and perhaps even the *emptiness* (phase 5) out of which the breathing seems to arise.

Metta

Mettā or one of the other *brahmavihāras* is another kind of home base.[12] We might repeat simple phrases that express friendliness or compassion: "May I be happy, free, and filled with ease. May you be filled with delight and ease,"

---

[12] The four brahmavihāras are *mettā* (friendliness), *karuna* (compassion), *muditā* (empathetic joy), and *upekkhā* (equanimity).

and so on. As we do this, we can focus on the *content* of the phrases (phase 1) or on the *process* of sending these qualities to ourselves or others (phase 2).

When I was practicing under the guidance of Bhante Vimalaraṁsi, he emphasized the *feeling* of kindness, compassion, etc. (phase 3). We might recall a time when it was strong and hold that quality in our hearts as it is radiated outward. As the qualities settle in, it is easier to notice the *expansiveness of awareness itself* (phase 4).

This practice is a little more difficult in the beginning than just watching the sensations of the breath or repeating a mettā phrase. But when it works, the meditation goes deeper because it begins in a more profound phase. Rather than beginning with physical sensations or words (phase 1), it begins higher up the spectrum with the quality of awareness (phase 3) and quickly moves to awareness itself (phase 4). And it's closer to awareness vanishing or "winking out" (phase 5).

Objectless Awareness

Objectless awareness is another home base, but it is unique in that it literally starts with nothing (phase 5). This is a very simple practice but very difficult because there is nothing to hang on to. We just start with a blank mind and if anything at all shows up (which it usually does), we treat it as a hindrance (*nīvaraṇa*) and work with it wisely and kindly.

These days my preferred meditation is just short of objectless awareness. There are many states that are right on the edge of objectless-ness. Chapter 6 (pp. 73-81) has a list of fourteen such signs of clear awareness. To meditate, we start by recalling one of these and how it feels. From there, we just relax toward objectless-ness.

Sometimes it's easy to do. Other times it is impossible because there is too much static in the mind. In this case, we either work with the distractions (nīvaraṇa) or temporarily use a practice that begins in an earlier phase.

Flexibility

Flexibility is implicit in using the Spectrum of Awareness in these ways. When someone is first learning meditation, rather than shifting techniques, it is usually helpful to adopt a simple practice and then work with it consistently. This allows the mind-heart to settle in without the potential distraction of deciding what to do while we're meditating.

However, with a lot of practice, we gradually become facile with techniques higher up the Spectrum. Earlier styles, such as watching content, may prevent the practice from going further. Instead, we shift up the Spectrum.

However, even with years of mastery, there may be days when there is just too much energy in our system. If we stay with subtler techniques, the mind just wanders off again and again until we become discouraged.

For intermediate and advanced practice it is helpful to be comfortable with several techniques. Then we can use the ones most appropriate for wherever the mind-heart finds itself on a given day.

Obviously, rapid shifts in practice are not helpful. Neither is sticking with something that is not working after a reasonable length of time. So, I encourage meditators who have some years under their belts to cultivate enough wisdom to recognize when it is best to stay with a given practice and when it is best to shift to a procedure in order to let the meditation practice deepen.

Having said that, the most advanced way to practice objectless awareness is to do nothing. This is both simple and difficult. If the mind is quiet, we do nothing but observe. If the mind is carrying on, we do nothing but observe. If the mind is nonobservant, we notice the nonobservance. The trick is to do this without migrating into the trance of thinking. Past and future fade as we quietly and openly receive the present.

Again, the core of meditation is to see what is most true from moment to moment. If we can recognize what's arising and passing and at the same time relax and expand, the mind will clear itself.

The practice of relaxing and expanding can be very subtle and nuanced. This is what makes it so effective. It can also make it difficult if the mind-heart is agitated, unruly, stubborn, or cranky — which it is all too often.

The Buddha had a solution for this as well. And that solution is the core of the practice he taught. I'll talk about that it in the next chapter.

5

The Three Ennobling Practices

Most scholars and students of Buddhism agree that the core of the Buddha's instructions is the so-called Four Noble Truths. I say "so-called" because in the Pāli language, the phrase is idiomatic. The "truths" are not philosophical principles but rather are three simple, specific observations. And "noble" doesn't refer to the observations but rather to the mind that sees them clearly and in so doing is ennobled.

So a better translation might be "the four ennobling observations." They enlighten us when we engage them skillfully. I refer to the first three as the Three Essential Practices because they are the core of the Buddha's practice. But let's look at all of them, beginning with the first observation and practice.

Dukkha

The first observation is *dukkha*. Dukkha has a range of meanings — suffering, dissatisfaction, dis-ease, stress — with no precise English equivalent. Literally the term refers to a wheel whose axle hole is slightly off center, causing it to press, rub, and wobble as it rotates.

Dukkha can be as intense as a cramp in our calf muscle or as gentle as a tickle on our cheek. It can be as complex as worrying about our children or as simple as wondering whether we put our dirty socks in the laundry. All these are dukkha: ways in which life rubs us the wrong way.

Our understanding of affective emotions (or any emotions) helps give texture and depth to this picture. We can think of emotion as "e-motion," where "e" stands for energy that puts us in motion. Affective emotions push or pull us into action. Without emotions, we'd potentially be little more than bumps on a log. For example, if we're hungry, we SEEK food. If we're tired, we SEEK rest. If we're lonely, we want CONNECTION. If someone we're fond of is hurting, we want to CARE for them.

Now we come to the crux of the matter: how do emotions motivate us to move in any given direction? They make us uncomfortable. They generate unease or suffering. They generate dukkha.

However, the affective emotions can certainly include sweet anticipation and other lovely feelings as well. Thus, when the Buddha spoke of the reality of suffering, he meant it is woven, in gross and subtle ways, into the fabric of our experience along with everything else. It's not that life *is* dukkha, only that it *includes* dukkha as it rolls along. To be more precise, it's not that *life* is dukkha. It's that *our responses to life* have dukkha embedded in them.

This is not our fault. We aren't to blame for this condition. Affective emotions have been wired into us through millions of years of evolutionary selection. We can't will them away. They are built into our systems.

And to take this one step further, as we saw in Chapter 2, neural science has found that, in normal circumstances, when all affective emotions go off line, *we* go off line. We go into a coma. This is true of all mammals and birds. If there is no need for us to do anything, there is no need for emotions. Without emotions, there is no dukkha. Without dukkha, awareness shuts down completely.

Does that sound depressing? Surely the Buddha didn't mean that dukkha is the only option! And it isn't. The fact that dukkha is so deeply and unavoidably a part of our experience is sobering. But there is a resolution: don't identify with experience. That is easier said than done. And it brings us to the core of the first practice.

Dukkha Is to Be Understood — Turning Toward

The first Essential Practice in the Buddhist text is "Dukkha is to be understood." By "understanding" he didn't mean an intellectual analysis. He meant deeply seeing the dynamics of suffering in our own experience: how dukkha arises, hangs around for a while, and then subsides. Without clear seeing, we get entangled in it. We end up identifying with dukkha rather than seeing it as a fleeting experience.

Since we often reflexively turn away from discomfort, I translate the first practice as "turning toward." We can't understand something if we refuse to see it. So, we turn toward dukkha and open up so that we might see its dynamics. The Buddha said that to be free, we have to know and understand the forces at play. Otherwise, we just get entangled in them.

Taṇhā

When we see dukkha at work, we see *taṇhā* or tension within it. The second observation is taṇhā.

Despite the mix and variety of dukkha and affective emotions, they all have physical, emotional, or mental tension. This might be felt as an inner push or pull or leaning. It might be felt as an emotional charge in our experience. This is simpler and easier to see when we turn toward rather than turn away.

Taṇhā Is to Be Abandoned — Relaxing Into

The second Essential Practice in the text is dramatic and straightforward: "*Taṇhā* is to be abandoned."

How do we abandon tension? We relax as fully as we can. In English, the word "relax" has a slightly negative connotation, as in "Relax man, let it go, get rid of it!" So I like to translate the second Essential Practice as "relaxing into." We relax into our hurt, hunger, loneliness, anger, or whatever disturbance might be there. This is a balanced movement of neither resisting nor indulging it. We let it be and just sit it in a relaxed, open way.

This doesn't necessarily get rid of the dukkha. But tension is the fuel that keeps dukkha puttering along. If we relax, the taṇhā may continue for a while. But without added straining, it soon runs out of gas.

Identification

One of the deepest and subtlest kinds of tension is identification. In this case we take our experience personally rather than seeing it as a result of impersonal causes and conditions. So abandoning taṇhā involves letting go of even the sense of self by relaxing into whatever experience rolls around. Relaxing pushes nothing away and grasps nothing. It just releases any charge within it.

As we saw in Chapters 3 and 4, the same effect can be had by letting our sense of self expand out into whatever feeling tone arises. We hold on to nothing and feel ourselves a part of everything — not separate. So *anattā* or nonself, is a subtle kind of relaxing-into and abandoning.

Seeing how deeply the affective and other emotions are wired into our brains can have the paradoxical effect of just letting them be as they are without holding or pushing anything away. The sense of the separate self that suffers starts to fade.

A number of years ago I went to see my therapist after a particularly difficult week. She listened kindly and attentively to my struggles. The difficult feelings subsided a little, but not completely. I said as much.

She sweetly replied, "Doug, it's only pain."

Something released inside me. Rather than sitting in a cauldron of pain, I began to be able to look at it from afar. I thought, "Yeah. That's right: it's only pain. What's the big deal?" I was no longer resisting the pain. With this, it lightened up immediately.

She wasn't saying I was bad or wrong for feeling hurt, the way my father had sometimes implied. She wasn't encouraging me to push anything away—only to turn toward it more deeply, understand it more fully, and relax into it more completely.

I think this is what the Buddha was encouraging us to do: to not try to rise above pain, but rather to transmute it by relaxing through it.

When we look at neural science, we get a slightly different view of the same phenomena as well as some additional hints as to how to work with them.

As we've seen, consciousness itself has its source in affective emotions, which come in fewer varieties and less detail than all of our feelings, stories, and thoughts.

Sometimes we can recognize primary affective emotions within those meandering thoughts and uncomfortable weavings. When we turn toward and relax into them, they can subside. That enables all the secondary and tertiary thoughts, stories, and feelings to lose their density and power. Even the sense of self itself starts to fade into the sunset, leaving behind a vast peacefulness that is not dependent on keeping anything at bay. This peace may expose a quieter tension hiding underneath, but we can then turn toward that and relax into it. Serenity deepens.

To use another metaphor, it's like cutting a tree down. We can start at the top and pull off each leaf, then each twig, then the small branches, then the main ones. This gets the job done.

Alternatively, we can simply cut through the trunk and the whole tree falls at once.

Turning toward and relaxing into the affective emotions is like cutting through the trunk. Primary affective emotions are said to be primary because all the secondary, tertiary, and quaternary branches and leaves draw substance through them. When they release and relax, everything that depends on them fades as well. It's more efficient. And I've found it's more effective.

But don't take my word for it. Give it a try. When you do, it may give rise to a third insight.

Nirodha

The third observation of the Buddha is nirodha.

Technically, nirodha is a sense of peace and ease that is so complete that awareness itself shuts down. It's what happens when primary affective emotions cease naturally.

But less technically, it can refer to the peace and ease I mentioned in the prior section: awareness doesn't shut off completely; rather we still feel genuine expansiveness.

And here's the thing: even though this sense of peace may be intermittent, the more we experience it, the more it seems as if it's been here all along. It was just so quiet that we missed it. But when we do open up to it, it feels like an old friend who was quietly present all along.

Neural science suggests (Chapter 3) one reason we may overlook the peacefulness: the brain and nervous system often seem to be biased toward negative experiences. I think the Buddha recognized this as well. So, whenever we are not in real danger, he encouraged us to give some extra attention to naturally positive feelings when they arise. This is the next practice.

Nirodha Is to Be Realized — Savor/Smile

In the text, the third Essential Practice is "Nirodha is to be realized." Here, "realize" means "to make it real." How do we "make something real"? We open up and let it soak in.

So I like to translate the third Essential Practice as "savor." We savor the good feelings when they arise. We let them soak into our bones. This helps balance out our evolutionary sensitivity to negative emotions.

And if the good feelings don't arise, we don't force it. Instead we can just bring up the corners of our mouth into a Buddha half smile. Neurologically, this tends to bring some ease and uplift to the mind-heart. But there is no need to force the feelings. Lifting the corners of the mouth is a reminder of that which is a little hidden at the moment.

This may seem to contradict what the Buddha said about dukkha being such an intrinsic part of life. But he didn't say it had to be that way. If we can genuinely release the charge of taṇhā, then we are relieved of suffering. Joy, peace, and contentment are unmasked. They were here all the time, lost in the fog, which just sensing them helps to lift. Then nirodha, or contentment, is realized.

Understanding the negativity bias makes it easier for us to realize the importance of the practice of savoring whenever we experience any genuine uplift. It helps us balance. It helps the wheel turn more smoothly.

The Eightfold Check List

The fourth Noble Truth is the so-called Eightfold Path. I say "so-called" because I think of it as an eight-part checklist rather than a linear path. If the first three practices are not working well, the Buddha suggested eight areas we can check to better tune our practice.

I have written about these elsewhere.[13] Since they are not as involved with the affective emotions, I'll just mention them here without going into detail. The first two are the most important:

(1) Wise view — seeing things impersonally

---

[13] *Buddha's Map* (2013), *Meditator's Field Guide* (2017), *Befriending the Mind* (2019).

(2) Wise intentions — these grow naturally out of taking things impersonally

It might also help to look at specific outward actions that are vulnerable to unwholesome states and make sure they are free of tension:

(3) Wise speech — being honest, open, supportive, truthful

(4) Wise action — not harming in our intentions and behavior

(5) Wise livelihood — doing no harm in how we support ourselves and our families

It also helps to look inwardly at our:

(6) Wise effort — making strong, and clear efforts without being forced

(7) Wise mindfulness — clearly seeing the qualities of our awareness

(8) Wise samadhi — inner collectedness

Beyond these eight, it can also be helpful to know our own unique blind spots and check on them. For example, my childhood left me with a proclivity toward cynicism: self-doubt comes easily for me. Sometimes I find it helpful to ask myself if I'm doing a little better than I realize. I don't assume I am. But knowing my own bias helps me to ask with clear eyes and an open heart.

Think about what your blind spots might be. Use self-knowledge to look at your personal biases openly.

6

Awareness Is Magic: Enlightened Futility

See simplicity in the complicated.
– Lao Tsu

Now we come to the core of the Buddha's teachings. This principle is not stated explicitly in the text, but it undergirds all his teachings. It is also not stated explicitly in neural science but is implied in its findings.

The principle is this: awareness is magic. Awareness is the ultimate healer of all that disturbs us. In the long run it dispels all dukkha.

Why does awareness heal? I have no idea. And if the Buddha knew, the answer wasn't passed down to us. Ultimately, I suspect there is no answer. Asking why awareness heals is like asking, "Why is there gravity? Why do large celestial bodies pull on other objects?" I have no idea. There's no explanation. It's just how human beings are made.

Physics can tell us how gravity works. Mathematical equations eloquently describe its effects. (It varies directly with the mass of the objects and inversely with the square of the distance between them.) But why do those formulas work? There's no reason. It's just how things are. Neural science cannot explain why awareness heals any more than physics can explain why gravity attracts.

When I say, "Awareness is magic," I'm not suggesting that it is supernatural or draws on occult forces. Quite the opposite. The healing power of awareness is as natural as gravity. It does not draw on any other force.

Buddhist practice ultimately rests on the seemingly magical healing power of awareness. The effects are subtle enough that they can be masked. The most obvious mask is tension. But ultimately, the practice is not even about getting rid of tension. It's about seeing it clearly. When tension and awareness are both present, awareness wins in the long run. Tension wears out and exhausts itself eventually. But with awareness, there is nothing to be worn out. It just is.

It's also said that awareness can be one insult after another. As we open up deeply, all the messy things we tried to bury rise to the surface, one insult after another. But the solution is to trust awareness: turn toward and relax into it.

Trying to fight, control, or ignore awareness is like trying to fight, control, or ignore gravity. Good luck with that! Gravity is there whether we acknowledge it or not. Awareness heals, whether we give it credit or not.

However, our practice and our living do improve over the long run if we accept awareness as it is. Spiritual practice is less about attaining and more about attuning to a deeper reality. And even if we get caught on the "attainment" treadmill, being aware of the treadmill is healing over the long run. Our lives do become easier if we accept things as they are.

Sometimes the ways we ignore reality can be subtle. For example, somebody attached comments to a Dhammā talk I have on YouTube. The person called me a "low caliber, verbose, disgusting, megalomaniac," and more. I thought it best to just ignore the insults. So I did. Or I tried to.

Yet, in quiet moments, I kept thinking of clever responses I could post like, "If you'd like to say what you disagree with, maybe we can have a conversation."

I asked a friend, "Do you think that's a good response?"

She smiled and shook her head. "No. It'll just enflame."

So I did nothing.

A few days later I woke up in the middle of the night thinking about a note Ralph Waldo Emerson sent to his brother Charles during the controversy over Transcendentalism in the early 1800s. Part of it said, "They say the world is vexed with us on account of our wicked writings. I trust it will recover its composure."

I thought, "That's brilliant. I could post that quote on YouTube. It would be a good poke in the eye of my YouTube detractor while I pretend to take the high road."

Then I caught myself: "Poke in the eye? Is this the affective emotion of RAGE?"

It obviously was. I don't like to admit rage, even to myself. But there it was. In my mind I heard the voice of my old therapist saying, "Doug, it's only RAGE."

Suddenly I was smiling. It was such a relief to let the feeling be what it was unconstrained by propriety. When I befriended inner RAGE rather than trying to ignore it, it peaked and subsided even if I didn't act on it.

"Is there anything hiding beyond the RAGE?" I wondered. Yes. There was a little bit of CONNECTION — or actually the loss of connection. I relaxed into that whiff of loneliness.

"Is there anything beyond the RAGE and missing CONNECTION?" No. Beyond them felt like endless space. Within five minutes, the RAGE and CONNECTION had faded into the distance and there was little except ease and a persistent smile. There was not even a definable self. Just open space.

In the days since, I have thought about my YouTube guy now and again. Each time, a soft smile arises.

Clear awareness is magic.

Enlightened Futility

Another way to say, "Awareness is magic" is "enlightened futility." We see deeply that trying to get somewhere in meditation can only get us so far. Eventually we hit a wall because of the tension of trying hinders awareness. Trying to get any farther ultimately doesn't work.

The only option left is to see starkly, sincerely, and unromantically exactly where the mind-heart is at this very moment. This is what I mean by "enlightened futility."

I was meditating in the wee hours of the morning when I noticed the song "America the Beautiful" was singing softly in the background of my mind. I was a bit annoyed by the intrusion and blocked it out. That left my mind with a stodgy block, not with the sweet stillness I had had earlier.

"Well, that didn't work so well," I thought. So, I relaxed and let the anthem sing itself. I let it be as it was. It came back and then slowly faded into a deeper stillness. All was quiet.

That is the magic of awareness. It's also radical acceptance and enlightened futility. They all point toward clear awareness.

Signs of Clear Awareness

If you have some inclinations toward skepticism or doubt, as I do, there are a few things we can do to take advantage of the magical healing power of awareness.

One is to notice the quiet, subtle effects of clear awareness — the signs that it is there in a relatively pure form. It is always present, though it is often elusive enough to slip by unacknowledged. But if we know some signs of it, it is easier to feel it sitting quietly in the shadows.

The signs are not states to strive for! That doesn't work. But if we sense them, it does help to relax into them and soak them up. This wears down the cynicism and at the same time helps the sense of self get a little rest.

Clear awareness is not monolithic or something that's either on or off. Rather, it's a collection of qualities that wax and wane on their own.

The following are a few signs of clear awareness that I notice. You may notice these as well or observe very different ones. We all have slightly different proclivities. You might want to use my list or make your own.

I have not listed them in any particular order because they emerge differently for different people.

Fading of Thoughts

The most obvious sign of clear mind is the fading of thoughts. Ordinary thoughts may include narratives, vignettes, dialogues, explanations, arguments, complaints, quiet conversations, gentle murmurs, and more. However, they all drift into the background as the mind feels more spacious.

This is not accomplished by intentionally stopping mental chatter. Rather we let the thoughts be without getting tangled up in them. Then they feel less relevant and drift away. We relax. Without tension, thoughts have no fuel and start to thin out.

A Feeling of Dropping

Often the fading of thought happens gradually. But sometimes it can happen rapidly. It's as if the mind has used up the tension that fuels it and it relaxes by itself. We feel the effects of gravity. It's a sensation similar to the body relaxing and dropping a little, but it's serene.

Loss of a Protagonist

Without stories, narratives, and dialogues, the sense of an inner self — a protagonist, if you will, the main character in our internal stories — slowly dwindles into irrelevance. Rather than being front and center, the self recedes into the background. In the foreground is a growing stillness.

It is generally not wise to try to get rid of the stories, narratives, or the protagonist. Such efforts just strengthen the sense of a lead character trying to control the inner space.

Instead, we observe them like a field naturalist watching animals without disturbing them. This allows us to see inner phenomena more lucidly. They seem like bubbles, or vortices (to use the Buddha's metaphors), that have surfaces but no underlying substance. They are constructs around a vacuum or activities around a stillness.

Rather than declaring "I am free," we see that there is no protagonist to be freed. There is nothing underneath in which to get entangled. That is freedom and disentanglement.

Loss of Solidity

The loss of narratives, stories, and protagonist may give rise to a loss of a sense of inner solidity. There may still be a weak sense of self, but it feels ephemeral. This is *anattā* — the beginning of nonself.

And it can arise in the opposite order, too — sometimes the sense of a solid self weakens, followed by the loss of stories, inner conversations, and all the rest.

Nondual Awareness

The fading of thoughts often gives rise to what could be called, "nondual awareness" in which logical opposites coexist peacefully. For example, as I accepted the RAGE about the YouTube guy, for a few moments I felt both anger and serenity. Opposites are not hobgoblins. We don't have to resolve seeming paradoxes. We let the thoughts be there and, at the same time, notice a serenity that feels like it's been there all along.

It's like a storm at sea. Trying to calm the waves by beating them down with a stick is futile at best. If anything, it just creates more turmoil. But if we go beneath the waves, there's already a stillness. It has been waiting for us patiently. And it's as big as the ocean itself.

Tingliness

One subtle but obvious physical sign of clear awareness is small waves of tingliness on the surface of the body. I used to call them "prickles." More often they are called "goosebumps." It feels like the skin is relaxing and the pores are opening. These gentle waves of sensation may flow through various parts of the body. If we relax into them, the waves may get bigger or infuse more of the body.

As the body relaxes, the brain often produces small amounts of dopamine and other neural transmitters. Tingliness may be one way they are felt. It's an impersonal, body response.

Content Fades into Process

The mind is constructed to know things that are happening. To give context to these happenings, it also puts them into larger stories.

Yet, as the mind quiets, these contexts and stories recede and fade into the background. Meanwhile, the processes become more prominent. We become more aware of what the mind is *doing* — e.g., thinking, worrying, explaining, complaining, musing, storytelling, and so on. The *content* of thinking and storytelling fades. Awareness shifts from nouns to verbs, from content to processes. Content is usually in the past or future while processes are acting in the present. The mind settles more and more into this present moment.

The shift from content to process is part of a meditation strategy (Chapter 4). However, sometimes content can fade into process on its own. The same thing can happen with the next three signs of clear awareness.

No-Thing

In the text, this fading of content into process is sometimes called "the realm of nothingness." But I think that is a mistranslation. It really means "no-thing-ness." Awareness itself doesn't stop. But it is relaxed enough that it doesn't coalesce into separate things. Ironically, there may still be a lot going on in no-thingness. But the mind doesn't perceive separate objects so much as the moment-to-moment flow of feelings and textures.

Process Fades into Qualities of Awareness

Years ago I noticed times when my mind seemed like a herd of buffalo raising clouds of dust as it stampeded across a distant prairie. The individual animals became indistinct while the feeling of rumbling became more prominent.

Just as awareness of content can give way to awareness of processes, awareness of processes can give way to awareness of qualities of awareness. Qualities include feeling tones or textures: rumbling, quiet, jumpy, smooth, spacious, thick, etc. There is a large variety of possible qualities. Noticing them is like noticing the mood of a story without paying attention to the characters or plot.

The quality of awareness is a phase of the Spectrum of Awareness (Chapter 4).

Qualities Fade into the Field of Awareness

Sometimes the qualities of awareness fade into the background, leaving a sense of presence that is open and empty. This is "awareness of awareness" because we sense awareness even as its contents and qualities are drifting away: we are aware of awareness itself even if there are no "things" in it.

Another way to say this is that everything outside the current moment feels less and less relevant. In the moment, there are no stories or things — just a quiet sense of presence.

To see this movement of attention from content to process to qualities to presence, consider another example. There are times in meditation when my mind gets antsy. I used to will up a strong determination to overcome the restlessness. I don't do that anymore. Now I just notice the agitation as a phenomenon. I notice how the mind wants to daydream and how the daydreaming can feel comforting compared to the agitation. So I let it daydream.

But here's the trick. Rather than focus on the content of the daydream or even the process of daydreaming, I notice the feeling of comfort that arises with the daydream.

The comfort is in the present. The content of the daydream is not. So I let the mind rest in the comfort. I savor it. With this, the mind tends to relax into the soothing feeling. The content drifts away. The daydreaming process slips away. And the mind settles into a comfortable abiding with very little going on.

This abiding is also part of the Spectrum of Awareness (Chapter 4).

Quiet Smile

In clear awareness, a quiet smile often sneaks up on me. I'm sitting in meditation. Suddenly I'm grinning widely though I hadn't seen that smile come up. At these times, the mind is usually bright, smooth, and a little surprised at how good it feels. When I first started noticing this years ago, I thought, "Where did that come from?" These days it's familiar enough that I no longer ask. If I relax into the smile, it goes deeper.

Sometimes I call this a "Buddha smile" because it's like the half smile we see on many statues of the Buddha.

Chuckles and Sighs

Sometimes a quiet chuckle or sigh arises spontaneously. Like the quiet smile, I usually don't see it coming. It just happens.

The diaphragm that powers our lungs is one of the larger and stronger muscles in the body. When we tense up, a lot of the tightness gets held in the diaphragm. As the muscle relaxes, it sometimes shakes reflexively to loosen up. Chuckles and sighs are the result of this dispersal of tension.

Body Posture Corrections

With clear awareness, the body is more likely to spontaneously adjust posture without comment. For example, if I'm sitting hunched over, the body may spontaneously elongate before I even think about it.

Soft Eyes

Along with this, the eyes tend to relax. The eyes, like the mind, become less interested in seeking what they want than in receiving what is already here. We may experience this as a physical softening of the eyes and their surrounding sockets.

Receptive Rather than Active

Like the softening eyes, we become content to receive whatever presents itself. We become more interested in attuning than attaining: attuning to what's here rather than attaining what is not here.

We become more interested in being than in doing. We're more interested in what is going on than in what we might want. We have less judgment and more curiosity. And eventually we have less curiosity and more presence.

Nimitta

Nimitta is a Sanskrit term for "sign." A visual nimitta is a sign of a relaxed, attentive awareness. When our eyes are closed, it may appear as a white, fuzzy area in the center of the field of vision. In the center of the retina (the fovea) there is a larger concentration of rods and cones (light receptors) than in the periphery. The nimitta phenomenon is probably the result of neural static from the denser concentration of light receptors in the fovea. We have to be deeply relaxed and receptive to see this effect. If we actively look for it, it will disappear.

Flickering Images

When the mind is clear, relaxed, and receptive, faint images may flash through the mind very quickly. The images have little charge to them and seem unrelated to one another.

While a nimitta is probably produced by the retina, the flickering images are probably produced by the brain itself. I suspect that, with 86 billion neurons, these quick flashes are faint static in the brain. Even a small amount of tension will blot them out.

"Of Course"

If I'm meditating with an unclear mind, meandering in thoughts, and realize what's going on, I'm likely to respond with an inner "Oh no," as in, "Oh no, my practice is messed up."

If I'm meditating with a clear mind that wanders into a thought and I realize what's going on, I'm likely to respond with an inner "Of course." This is an acceptance that given what my mind has been through that day or in recent days, of course it drifted. I take it impersonally and with a light spirit.

To say it differently, I'm more likely to just let things be and trust the magic of awareness to fine-tune the mind rather than trying to push it into some semblance of a "better" state.

Relaxing Into or Spreading Out

When awareness is clear enough, the "Of course" may not even arise. If a bit of tension comes into the body, it may reflexively relax. The body softens without us even thinking about it.

Without clear awareness, my first response to tension is likely to be tensing up further. But with clear awareness the tightness tends to dissolve on its own.

Emptiness of Time and Space

Emptiness of time and space is a sign that often arises with the other signs I've already mentioned. Time and space may not completely disappear at first. They just seem irrelevant. They have no draw.

However, the emptiness of time or space can also be a "leading indicator" that appears first and helps usher in other signs. Particularly if you are working with the expansiveness described earlier (Chapter 2), the loss of a sense of time and space can arise all by itself.

Blank Spots

The final sign of clear awareness that I'll mention is subtle and potentially confusing. Sometimes we may experience blank spots in immediate short-term memory. These are part of the "Nothingness" phase of the Spectrum of Awareness.

It takes a little effort to remember what just happened. When the awareness gets completely relaxed, it may stop registering experiences or stop putting them into memory. The result is a blank spot in memory. Usually we don't even notice these. Or if we do, we think we must have fallen asleep. But if the mind is bright and clear rather than groggy, the mind probably did not go unconscious. It just turned off its inner recorder, leaving an empty moment.

Implications for Meditation

Again, these various signs of clear awareness are not separate; they overlap in many ways. Not experiencing them is not necessarily a sign of bad practice. And you may experience other things you associate with clear awareness that I have not mentioned.

By outlining these I do not intend to turn them into practices to be pursued diligently. I describe them in case you have noticed some of them in your own experience. If, like me, you are sometimes skeptical of your meditative skills, you can use these as encouragement that you may be doing better than you think. It's okay to relax and get out of the way.

And by lightly turning toward your own experiences, you may create the "causes and conditions" in which they are more likely to arise again. After all, they are with us all the time anyway. Noticing them attunes us to them and helps them quietly strengthen. Recalling how they feel without lifting a finger to conjure them up creates the conditions in which they are more likely to arise spontaneously. It makes us more receptive.

High Altitude Meditation

Clear awareness and signs of nirodha are hints of what could be called "high altitude meditation." They are close to the peak of the metaphorical meditation mountain. As stable experiences, they are statistically rare. There are hundreds of people at lower elevations but few regularly this high up.

Nevertheless, over the years of mentoring meditators I have found that many people have fleeting yet genuine glimpses of these upper reaches. At first the experiences are not stable. They are subtle and may pass through with little notice.

However, if they do notice them and know how to adjust their meditation to take advantage of them, they can be a great boon.

Two techniques that leverage clear awareness and glimpses of nirodha could be called "clear mind" or "awareness of awareness" and "empty mind" or "objectless awareness. They are the upper phases of the Spectrum of Awareness (Chapter 4) and the higher jhānas, particularly the Base of Neither Perception nor Non-Perception.[14] They utilize some of the magical qualities of awareness.

An analogy suggests what these techniques have in common and how they differ:

My little home office has a desk in the corner, several chairs, file cabinets, a throw rug, shelves, lots of books, huge dust bunnies hidden behind a computer screen, cough drop wrappers in the wastebasket, etc. I could bring more accoutrements into the room until it's as congested as a packrat's nest. I could also remove clutter until the room is as spare as a Zen monk's kuti. But no matter how much or how little is in my office, the room has the same walls, windows, doors, floor, and ceiling. The room itself is not altered by the presence or absence of content.

Awareness of Awareness

Beginning and intermediate meditations utilize the contents of awareness to help settle the mind. Most focus on a single, primary object: the breath, a mantra, mettā, equanimity, etc. We are taught to attend to this one object and ignore everything else. This is like putting a little statue on my desk and focusing on it to the exclusion of everything else.

---

[14] I describe the jhānas in more detail in *Buddha's Map* (2013).

But at higher elevations, the instructions shift. We can ignore *all content* and just be aware of the room itself. It doesn't matter whether there's a lot in in the room or not. We just shift our attention from the paraphernalia (or lack of it) to the room itself. In actual meditation this means shifting awareness from the content of the mind to the awareness that is noticing the content. This often feels like a figure-ground shift as attention goes from a primary object to awareness of awareness itself.

The contents don't automatically disappear. They just fade into the background as we notice the awareness itself. With more practice, the bric-a-brac in the background may quietly fade completely due to lack of attention. But we are not concerned with whether they are there or not.

This practice has been called "clear mind" or "awareness of awareness." The clear mind often has a slightly luminous quality. So it's also been called "clear light awareness" and "luminous mind." It seems to flow out in all directions.

Objectless Awareness

As practice goes deeper, awareness fades altogether and we can engage the second technique called "empty mind." It has also been called "objectless awareness," "meditating on emptiness," "emptiness of emptiness," and "nothingness."

Note: This nothingness should not be confused with the base of nothingness in the upper jhānas. As we saw earlier in this chapter, in the jhānas, "nothingness" might be better translated as "no-thing-ness" because the flow of experience does not separate into distinct things. As perception relaxes and fades, experiences gently blend together rather than present as discrete objects. Ironically, there may be a lot going on in the base of no-thing-ness. But there are no separate things.

However, in empty mind or objectless awareness there is truly nothing, not even a flow of experience. We're aware of emptiness. The room itself is gone and the mind relaxes in nothingness. When awareness is not perfect (which is most of the time) objects will arise: thoughts, images, impulses, feelings, and more. But if we try to Six-R these or even relax them, the effort of trying is too coarse. It brings more disturbance. However, doing nothing lets awareness itself release any tension. The most helpful thing we can do is get out of the way and let the awareness dissolve anything that arises.

In his book *Progressive Stages of Meditation on Emptiness* (2016), Lama Tsultrim Gyamtso describes five different kinds of practices at this highest level of meditation. He writes:

> *By the time one comes to meditation based on the Clear Light Nature of the Mind, the investigation stage of the practice has come to an end. All there is to do now is to rest the mind naturally in its own nature, just as it is without any contrivance or effort. … [W]hatever thoughts arise, there is no need to try to stop them; in that state they simply liberate themselves. It is like waves on an ocean that simply come to rest by themselves. No effort is required to still them.*[15]

Lama Gyamtso's five meditations on emptiness come from different schools of Buddhism. Each stage goes a little deeper than the one before it. And most stages have substages. I suspect that many of the differences between the five have more to do with differences in cultures, languages, and personalities than fundamental differences in practice. After all, no two brain neural networks are the same. How each of us processes subtle information varies.

---

[15] Khenpo Tsultrim Gyamtso Rinpoche and Lama Shenpen Hookham, *Progressive Stages of Meditation on Emptiness* (Shrimala Trust, 2016), p. 104.

It's as if we are walking through the woods and come upon two trees. Are they different enough to be different species? Or are they different varieties of the same species? Or just different views of the same tree? I suspect Lama Gyamtso's five practices are different varieties of awareness and emptiness.

What's most important in all of them is shifting awareness from the objects to awareness itself and from awareness of awareness to emptiness. As we do this, it helps to relax all effort to do anything. We just get out of the way and let awareness do the work of dissolving the last vestiges of tension.

That is the magic power of awareness to relax and heal.

What I find tricky in using these techniques is sorting out when a little bit of relaxation is still skillful practice and when awareness is clear and deep enough to do nothing. If I try to figure this out while meditating, the cogitation activates perception, memory, and cognition. They are coarser and heavier than clear mind or objectless awareness. They create enough disturbance that I fall back into the room of objects at lower elevations.

This is where the signs of awareness described in this chapter can be so helpful. If they are arising, then I know awareness is dissolving tension. There is nothing I need to do. It's time to simply and patiently get out of the way.

One final note: Khenpo Tsultrim Gyamtso Rinpoche suggests not going straight to objectless awareness. Rather, he recommends going to clear mind. This is where there is nothing but awareness quietly flowing out in all directions. In time, if we simply rest there, in time empty mind or objectless awareness arises on its own.

However, I have noticed that with advanced meditators it is often easy and less complicated to just go to objectless awareness. If the mind does not settle into emptiness, then we can go to clear awareness for a while.

What's most important is not trying to push, guide, or even gently lead the mind. Instead we attune to it. If we take care of awareness by attuning to it, awareness will take care of us by letting us dissolve.

That is freedom.

7

Homeostasis: Pain and Pleasure as Messengers

In classical Buddhism, the sources of our misery are greed, hatred, and delusion. The Pāli terms are *lobha, dosa,* and *moha.* They can be translated less flamboyantly as "liking," "disliking," and "confusion." Together they are deemed "the three poisons." Nobody likes poison. So the implication is that if we could expunge them from our system, our emotional and spiritual health would greatly improve.

Greedy Squirrel

In theory, that is undoubtedly true. But in practice, hating our greed and hatred or disliking our liking and disliking doesn't work. It just adds another dose of poison to the poisons. It makes them worse — not a winning formula.

Better formulas may come from better translations. English has an average of about twenty-five words for every word in Pāli. So Pāli terms have to cover a much broader range of meanings. Lobha could be translated as "yearning" or "inclination" rather than "greed," and dosa could be translated as "ennui" or "annoyance" rather than "hatred."

The Jesuits were the first to translate Pāli into English. While I have a lot of respect for them, they were taking a language that was new to them and translating it into the Bible's King James English. The words they chose were more moralistic and extreme than the Buddha's teachings.

I wish we could just drop their translations, but they are so familiar that forgetting them can be difficult. Lobha and dosa arise in response to things that bring us pleasure or pain. So, rather than dropping the language, it might be easier to find new metaphors that shift the emphasis away from the extremes of greed and hatred and toward a balanced response to pleasure and pain. After all, the Buddha did say the essence of his path is a "middle way."

The overarching concept of homeostasis might be a better way to think about these issues. Rather than trying to rid our brains of these words that carry a sense of negative judgment, it may be kinder and wiser to think of them in terms of homeostasis, or "pleasure and pain as messengers." Feelings of imbalance are helpful when they encourage us to take better care of our health or wellbeing or to turn away from harm. But there's no wisdom in killing the messenger.

The term "homeostasis" was coined in 1930 by the physician Walter Cannon. He combined the Greek words for "similar" and "standing still" into the idea of "staying the same." It refers to any process that maintains relatively stable internal conditions that allow the organism to survive. Without homeostasis we die.

Ava, Bea, and Cindy

To get an intuitive feel for how this works, envision three people sitting on a log by a river in a primeval forest a few hundred thousand years ago. We'll call them Ava, Bea, and Cindy. Each has a different way of perceiving and responding to what life presents.

At the moment, Ava feels that her blood glucose is low, feels dryness in her mouth and tongue, and senses her body temperature is below normal. But she is at peace with things just the way they are. Nothing disturbs her contentment.

Bea has no idea what her body metrics are. But she relishes eating fish, delights in drinking from the river, and enjoys warm clothes. She is disgruntled with the way things are and her instincts tell her what to do about it.

Cindy knows she feels hungry, thirsty, and cold but isn't confident of specific solutions. She's trying to figure them out.

If this snapshot is typical of Ava, Bea, and Cindy, then which of the three is likely to live the longest? Who is most likely to pass their genes on to the next generation?

Obviously, Ava is least likely to reproduce. We may envy her inner peace, but her sense of ease makes it possible for her to sit on a log and serenely waste away. Her genes would be removed from the gene pool.

There are some people who don't experience pain because of a rare neurological condition. Like Ava, they don't do very well in the long run. Without innate reflexes to avoid bodily harm, they are more likely to get burned, cut, or injured. Or they might sit on a log and slowly starve, dehydrate, or get ill from hypothermia while feeling no motivation to do anything about it.

In a stable environment with ample fish, streams, and clothing, Bea probably is the most likely to live long enough to produce offspring. She may not be as happy as Ava, but evolution doesn't care about feeling good as much as it does staying alive long enough to procreate. However, her instincts are specific. If the river dries up, she may be at a loss as to what to do.

In an unstable environment, Cindy and her children have the best chances for long lives. She might be the least happy of the three, but she is the most adaptable. In a stable environment she will not be as content as Bea, because it takes her longer to figure out what to do. But when the world is in flux, her flexibility gives her an edge over the long haul. Today, we are more likely to have her genes than those of Ava or Bea.

Befriending Lobha, Dosa, and Moha

If we don't care about staying alive, then getting rid of lobha, dosa, and moha is attractive. But if we do care, there are several other problems with eliminating them.

First, the terms "greed," "hatred," and "delusion" are moralistic. We're more likely to feel put down than to recognize the subtleties of our experience. As we saw earlier, disliking our disliking and liking may make things worse rather than better.

Second, the terms describe the most extreme manifestations of each and hardly even hint at the Buddha's middle way. As students of our own emotions, if we're primarily focused on banishing such extreme feelings to the wilderness, we may be distracted from seeking out a balance.

Third, living organisms have real homeostatic needs that must be addressed on their own terms if they are to continue to live. When we focus on the intensity of lobha, dosa, and moha, we can overlook the context and the content.

Different needs have different resolutions. For example, if we are hungry, rest will not help. If we're tired, a sandwich doesn't necessarily address our fatigue. If we're lonely, a workout may be a distraction but not a solution. And if we need exercise, talking to someone about it doesn't help us physiologically.

On the other hand, the relative intensities of feelings can be important. If I'm hungry and having trouble breathing, it's best to take care of the breathing first. The affective emotions will put a stronger valence on getting air. And that's a good thing!

Fourth, pleasure and pain refer to physical sensations while greed, hatred, and confusion refer to psychological reactions to pleasure and pain. It's hard to know for sure what the Buddha intended when he used the terms "lobha," "dosa," and "moha." It's easy to imagine his intended meaning drifting over the course of the hundreds of years it was transmitted orally among his followers. Unfortunately, today he's not around to clarify it for us.

While we tend to like what is pleasant and dislike what is painful, this is not always the case. For example, consider stretching in the morning. If our muscles are stiff and numb, it hurts to stretch them. But it also feels good to loosen them up. Most people don't hate stretching or yoga.

I will use "pleasure" and "pain" as the most helpful descriptions of what a homeostatic balance and imbalance feels like. This is closer to the physiological messages that alert us to problems.

Fifth, if we treat them as messengers and friends, an awareness of pleasure and pain can help us navigate our complex, multidimensional world. Again, there's no need to kill the messenger. Nor do we want to identify with the message. Instead, we can accept the information without taking it personally. It is beneficial to value and befriend our pleasure and pain so that we can relate to them with kindness and wisdom.

It may not always be easy. But it's workable. And in the long run, it's the only viable path toward surviving and thriving. The concept of homeostasis may be a better guide on that path than the old moralistic terms, for it plays an important role in keeping us alive and conscious. To see this, let's step back and put it into the larger frame of reference of what it means to exist as living, conscious beings. We'll start with simple existence.

Existence Requires Boundaries

What does it mean to say something "exists" — whether it be a rock, a whirlpool, or even us?

The most basic meaning is that there is a boundary or border between that thing and everything else.[16] There is a boundary between the rock, whirlpool, or me and the rest of the world. And what's inside each differs significantly from what's "out there."

The rock's border is its smooth surface. What's inside is more homogenous than the forest around it. The whirlpool's boundary is ambiguous — it's hard to tell exactly where the whirlpool ends and the surrounding river begins. But there is a boundary, even if it is imprecise. The water moves differently inside the vortex than it does in the rest of the river. My border

---

[16] Anil Seth, *Being You* (Penguin Random House, 2021), p. 205.

is my skin. Everything inside my epidermis is me. And my innards are different in many ways from the world around me.

Here's another way to view boundaries and differences: I have blue food coloring in an eyedropper and clear water in a glass. The coloring and water have boundaries and differences. Yet, if I squirt the coloring into the water, it disperses until they are indistinguishable. They cease to exist as separate things.

If I drop a little olive oil into the glass of water, it spreads out into a tiny disk on top of the water. It changes shape. But there is still a boundary between the oil and water that keeps them apart. They continue to exist separately.

The whirlpool is an intriguing example. It exists apart from the river because it moves differently than the river. But it takes energy to maintain the swirling. If that energy is expended, the spinning disappears, and the whirlpool blends with the river and ceases to exist as a distinct thing.

Since the spinning will eventually stop, the whirlpool has no permanent existence. It arises out of causes and conditions — i.e., currents in the river. When the supporting movements (the energy from the river) cease, the vortex disappears. It no longer exists.

In describing a vortex, the Buddha said a discerning person sees that the nature of the whirlpool is to dissolve into nothing. He said that our existence is like the whirlpool: temporary.

However, we are alive and the whirlpool is not, even if it has a boundary and movement. What does it mean, therefore, to say that something is alive?

Aliveness Requires Work

The most basic criterion for aliveness is that a living organism works to maintain its boundaries and to keep its essential variables within their homeostatic ranges. These inner ranges are usually narrower than in the larger world.

Nonliving objects may have boundaries and essential variables as well, but they do nothing to maintain them. The rock is completely passive. Its smooth surface and hard interior resist the forces of erosion. But it does nothing to maintain its rock-ness. Eventually it erodes or breaks or gets ground to dust and ceases to exist. It might stay intact for centuries or millennia, but it isn't alive.

The whirlpool is also passive. It receives energy from the river, but it does nothing to increase or even maintain those currents. It isn't alive.

My body, on the other hand, actively maintains its boundaries and works hard, both consciously and unconsciously, to keep its essential variables within their homeostatic ranges. Physical variables include body temperature, blood pressure, heart rate, breathing tempo, blood oxygen concentration, hydration, and much more. If too many variables go out of their limits for too long, I die. As the neural scientist Anil Seth puts it, eventually "I" will "turn to mush."[17]

I also have lots of nonphysical essential variables, such as social contact (too much and I get stressed; too little and I get lonely), activity (too much and I get worn out; too little and my muscles atrophy), mental stimulation (too much and I'm restless or frazzled; too little and I'm uninspired or bored), and so on. If too many of these go out of bounds for too long, I become a mess.

---

[17] Ibid, p. 206.

Being actively engaged in the business of staying alive is complex and makes us fragile. It requires more energy than the rock's passive resistance and more engagement than the whirlpool's laissez-faire. We have to extract fuel from the world around us and convert it into energy we can use: we have to eat, digest, drink, breath, metabolize, and so forth.

When I was first studying homeostasis and the amount of work required to maintain it, I found it confusing. Complex organisms have a lot more homeostatic systems than simpler organisms like insects or worms. We require more work and more energy to stay alive.

Rather than putting more and more work into complex systems, why doesn't evolution force us to simplify and do less? Wouldn't this make us more resilient during lean times? Wouldn't we have a better chance of surviving and reproducing in the long run?

The answer is "not necessarily."

Doing a lot of work to keep one essential variable within a narrow range can reduce the energy needed by other homeostatic processes. What counts in the long run is the total energy needed by the whole organism. If doing extra work to keep one process in balance means less work on other processes, over all there is less work to be done. It's an energy win for the whole organism.

For example, consider body temperature. Cold-blooded reptiles can stay intact within a much wider range of internal temperatures than most mammals and birds. Yet we're considered more evolved than lizards and turtles. How does that work?

If we keep our body temperature inside a narrow range, it makes digestion simpler: we don't have to digest material that is sometimes thicker when it's cold or thinner when it's warm.

If we keep our body temperature inside a narrow range, it's easier to maintain healthy tissue. Greater heat might make tissue softer and easier to tear. Greater cold might make it stiffer and less flexible. A constant body temperature means the tissues stay healthier.

If we keep our body temperature inside a narrow range and infecting microbes make us sick, the body can raise its temperature for a short time to kill off the organisms. Once they are gone, the body can drop back to its normal range. If the body temperature was normally within a broader range, then any infecting microbes would probably tolerate a broader range as well. This elegant defense mechanism wouldn't work.

And so forth.

Our complex bodies have hundreds of homeostatic variables. The interactions between one homeostatic system and all the rest can be quite complex. But if, overall, putting more energy into maintaining one system (such as body temperature) means needing less energy to maintain the entire organism, the total energy needed to stay alive is less. This gives us an evolutionary edge.

The same considerations apply to behavior. If a wolf can travel faster, farther, and for a longer period than a lizard or a snake, it will expend more energy. But if that makes it more efficient at hunting for food, it is a net gain. In a competition between a lizard and a wolf, I'd bet on the wolf. It is more adept at maintaining its homeostatic balances.

While wolves, lizards, and snakes are alive and conscious to some degree, there are some organisms that are not. What does it mean to say that an organism is "conscious"? And what's the relationship between homeostasis and consciousness?

These are the topics of the next chapter.

8

Consciousness Is Born: Complexity Is the Midwife

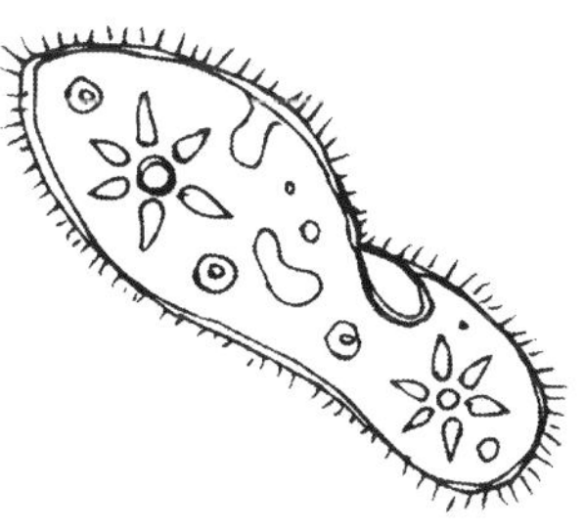

A paramecium is a very simple creature: one cell, a few organelles that help it along, and not much else. Like all living things, it must maintain homeostatic balances or die. But I doubt that it is conscious. Maintaining homeostatic balances in food and hydration requires action, but the paramecium doesn't cogitate about these, nor does it need to. It stays alive through instincts unmediated by thought. Its behaviors are driven by genes and inherited unconscious behaviors.

How did our consciousness evolve out of such blind, automated reflexes? We can only speculate. But I suspect that complexity gave rise to consciousness. Here's how:

As simple organisms evolved into multifaceted creatures, they acquired more homeostatic balances to be managed simultaneously. Inevitably, several conflicting imbalances arose at once, pushing the creature in different directions and causing it to vacillate or freeze up. Neither vacillation nor freezing helped it get by. And even when there were no direct clashes, resolving one imbalance might require putting another on hold for a while. Does the creature chase food, scratch an itch, get a drink, seek a mate, take a nap, build a nest…?

Developing new instincts through natural selection required many generations, while the situations they were coping with required quick solutions. If they were to flourish, they needed a whole new mechanism to deal with these complexities.

While we don't yet know exactly what happened, we can speculate that the conflicting instinctual reflexes created an internal stalemate out of which consciousness arose to sort out what to do next. It was a pause in which the equivalent of a mental space gradually opened up inside. Old vacillating or frozen reflexive actions became feelings of discomfort. Unfelt, genetically driven reflexes evolved into felt conscious pain. Pain, in turn, *encouraged* movement *without forcing* action. Different homeostatic needs created different feelings that coexisted uncomfortably. But the creature had latitude to decide what to do next.

Consciousness had emerged! The instincts to move were felt. Pain arose from unresolved homeostatic imbalances, and pleasure arose as balances were restored.[18]

At first the resolution of those feelings may have been as simple as the fact that the strongest won. Then, once the first

---

[18] An ancient believe suggests that consciousness can exist outside of the material world. Hence, when we die, we might go to heaven, hell, purgatory, be reborn in another body, enter a different realm, or some other possibility. I'm suggesting here that consciousness emerges out of matter itself, and hence there is no afterlife. But this is speculation. I don't think we have enough evidence yet to settle this debate definitively one way or another.

homeostatic imbalance was resolved, the next imbalance could be resolve, followed by the third, and so on.

Also, once there was even a little pause inside, the animal could consider what was available in the environment outside as well as what it felt inside. If it was thirsty but saw a predator coming its way, it could delay the drink until it got to safety.

Walking on the Shore

We humans have vastly more complex brains than those early, minimally conscious creatures. We have a large repertoire of homeostatic systems. But our underlying dynamics are the same, even if our consciousness and decisions are more intricate.

For example, imagine I'm walking with an old friend along the shore. A week of rain and drizzle left us feeling housebound. But now it's a lovely, sunny day and I'm enjoying my friend. After a while I get hungry and tired.

I'm drawn in several directions at once. I'd like some food, but we didn't bring any with us and leaving the beach would mean leaving the fresh air and open seascape I've wanted for days. I'd also like to rest, but the wind is chilly and it may be too cold to sit outside. I could talk all this through with my friend, but at the moment he's sharing deeply moving events and I'd like to hear him out.

How do I decide what to do?

Notice that several of the primordial affective emotions we met in Chapter 2 have been activated. There is SEEKING of food, rest, fresh air, and open scenery. There is CONNECTION in friendship. My friend's stories might elicit FEAR or RAGE (toned down into annoyance). There is CARE because of the tender topics he's sharing. There might even be some quiet PLAY as we amble along throwing seashells into the waves.

These are all homeostatic needs to be regulated.

Like the paramecium, we too have homeostatic needs that we don't think about. They operate unconsciously "under the hood," maintaining heart rate, blood flow, respiration, and more. We are continually making many, many more homeostatic adjustments than we're aware of. And that's a good thing! If we had to consciously manage them all, we'd be overwhelmed.

Fortunately our system handles most essential variables without conscious intent or will. But being the complex organisms that we are, there are a few that can't be managed by instinct alone. As noted, developing new instincts takes many generations and we often have just a few minutes to sort out what to do next.

Nature gave us a different mechanism to handle circumstances that need a quick resolution: consciousness. Affective emotions are the evolutionary invention that helps us navigate complex environments. And they are the source of consciousness.

As we saw earlier, affective emotions have a valence or intensity for each homeostatic imbalance. They vary in strength depending on the situation and our homeostatic needs. In choosing an action, the stronger feelings often win, but not always. To understand the nuances of this process, it helps to distinguish between exteroception, interoception, and affective emotions.

Exteroception, Interoception, and Affective Emotions

Exteroception is about what's going on "out there." It uses stimuli from outside the body to discern the world around us. It helps us know objects and movements in our vicinity.

Interoception is what's going on "in here." It uses stimuli from inside the body to discern heart rate, breath rate, hunger, and so forth. It gives us a broad, though sometimes fuzzy, felt sense of how our life is going "in here" — that is, inside the body.

Affective emotions are part of interoception. They tell us what we feel about what's going on "inside our lives." They aren't so much metrics of heart rate or blood pressure. They are much broader than just the objective physiological processes. They sort out how well or unwell our life is going. When we ask ourselves how we feel inside, usually we're not referring to our stomach or spleen or other organs. We're asking how we feel about our unfolding life.

Affective emotions tell us our mood in the moment without forcing us to do anything. By extension, they tell us how good or bad we might feel going forward on various paths. It doesn't make the choice for us but instead gives us emotional information and turns the decision over to us.

We, in turn, can weigh the strength of those various affective emotions. We can also take into account what opportunities are available to us.

For example, if there are vendor stands nearby, I might choose to get the food right away and continue our walk. If there is no food available on the beach, I might decide to tolerate the hunger and continue walking. If the forecast calls for more rain in the next few days, that may incline me to want to stay out longer today despite the chill. If the forecast calls for warm, dry weather tomorrow, I might prefer to cut our walk short and plan to come back the next day.

All this brings free will into the picture. I'm not forced to decide what to do. Instead, I'm given emotive information to weigh in making decisions. In Chapter 13, we will come back to free will versus determinism in more detail (p. 188).

To put a fine point on it, I can't decide what to feel. That just happens. But I can decide what to do or not do about what I feel. And what I do may influence how I feel about it in the next moment. While I can't dictate to myself what to feel, I can create the causes and conditions that will themselves influence how I'll feel later. The feeling may push me in one direction or another, but I retain some freedom in making that choice.

Also notice that while exteroception, interoception, and affective emotions sound like they belong in the same family, they have very different personalities. Exteroception gives us sharply defined objects "out there." Interoception gives us fuzzy feeling tones about how it's going "in here" in our life. Exteroception tells us about tangible stuff. Interoception tells us about intangible feeling tones without telling us exactly what's physically going on inside. They just show us moods about what we are doing.

As noted in Chapter 2 (pp. 11-16), affective emotions are the source of consciousness itself. I don't say this just because it makes sense to me (which it does). I say it because we know that when the areas of the brain that process affective emotions are turned off or removed, consciousness is usually turned off and removed. We go into a coma. The evidence is empirical.

Mystery of Consciousness

After reading this far, if consciousness and its origins still seem a little mysterious to you, I'm with you. There are parts of it that remain enigmatic to me as well.

It's important to distinguish between self-consciousness (as in being anxiously over aware of our appearance or actions) and consciousness itself. Yet, as Anil Seth[19] puts it, without a sense of self, it is probable that there is consciousness. I suspect he's right.

Taking another tack, the American philosopher Thomas Nagel, famously asked, "What is it like to be a bat?"[20] If we can say what it's like to be something, there must be consciousness. For example, we can imagine what it's like to be a dog with a ball or a bird looking down at us from a tree. On the other hand, it's hard to imagine what it might be like to be the ball or the tree. Therefore, the dog and bird are probably conscious while the ball and tree are not.

However, Nagel's question is about presence or absence of consciousness, not a definition of it. To have a sense of what it's like to be a dog or bird doesn't describe exactly what consciousness is.

Analogously, if asked what green is, we could easily say, "It's the color of a banana tree leaf or the color of grass in the spring." These examples are fine, but they are examples of the color, not a definition of it.

So we might try again and say with great precision, "Green is the electromagnetic wavelengths of 495 to 570 nanometers."

---

[19] Anil Seth, *Being You* (New York: Penguin Random House, 2021), p. 34

[20] This essay first appeared in *The Philosophical Review,* October 1974 and again, later, in *Mortal Question* (1979).

But that scientific designation tells us nothing about the actual experience of green.

In this chapter I've speculated about the evolutionary origins of consciousness. Once there were animals who, for example, had automated reflexes to search out and drink water when their hydration levels were low. And many generations later, their descendants felt a desire for water when they were parched. Somewhere in the generations between the great, great grandparents and their great, great grandchildren, the reflex turned into a felt sense of thirst. It became conscious.

But we still do not know the precise physiological mechanisms that turned the unconscious reflex into a conscious experience.

The cognitive psychologist Donald Hoffman speculates that the reason we have been unable to pin down how consciousness arises out of physical matter is because it doesn't. In his book *The Case Against Reality,*[21] he suggests we have the causal relationship backward: our perceptions of the world may be a byproduct of our consciousness rather than a source of it. He refers to the conventional, three-dimensional world we assume to be the bedrock of reality as an interface between consciousness and a vastly more complex real world.

To elucidate this interface theory, he proposes the analogy of a computer desktop. My desktop has many icons. Before typing these words, I double-clicked a little square on the desktop above the label "Presence." The desktop filled with other icons (words and letters). And now I'm typing away to create more symbols.

---

[21] Donald Hoffman, *The Case Against Reality: Why Evolution Hid the Truth from Our Eyes* (New York: W. W. Norton, 2019)

The reality of all this seems simple and obvious. But it's an illusion. The real physical nature of this book is composed of variations in electrical voltages inside transistors and other electronic components inside a little box behind my computer screen. On top of this hardware are many layers of software through which electrons flow. If I had to consciously manipulate those voltages and layers of software, I'd probably be overwhelmed and opt for a quill and paper to do my writing.

The icons are illusions that obscure more intricate items behind them. This doesn't mean that I'm completely hallucinating. There is a real world. And if I drag the little "Presence" rectangle to the trashcan icon, my work will indeed be lost. But the destruction process is vastly more complicated than a trash icon.

Hoffman suggests that the time-space continuum that seems so real and solid is similar to a simplified desktop that allows us to navigate a more complex world. This interface helps us stay alive and raise our children. Consciousness creates our perceptions of a three-dimensional world that makes it easier for us to pass our genes on to the next generation. Perception wins not by showing us the real world but by helping us navigate it more effectively. When we look around, we see the simplified interface rather than the real, undisguised, physical world.

Since the sensory organs and biological imperatives vary from species to species, different species perceive different worlds. Even between members of the same species, our desktops are not identical. The worlds we live in are not the same.

I find Hoffman's interface theory mindboggling. But the world of quantum mechanics and subatomic particles is also boggling. The hood of a car is vastly different from the contents of the engine compartment that it covers. Quantum mechanics may be a peek beneath the hood of our interface. In quantum mechanics, the laws of the conventional world do not operate as we expect: time can flow backward; entangled subatomic particles separated by hundreds of light-years can respond to each other faster than the speed of light; and so on.

None of this proves that consciousness is primary and that conventional space-time is a secondary derivative. Or vice versa.

Hoffman's interface theory resonates with Plato's twenty-five-hundred-year-old allegory of the cave in which prisoners are chained in such a way that they could not see themselves. A fire projects their shadows onto the cave wall. They mistake these two-dimensional images for the whole of reality.

The Buddha lived about one hundred years before Plato. But the Buddha cannot help us unravel the mystery of consciousness either. He was not interested in philosophical, intellectual, or even scientific questions. His focus was on the relief of suffering. He said that liking, disliking, and confusion are the source of suffering. And we can surmise that they are tied up in consciousness: they are things we feel.

But the Buddha was a phenomenologist, not a philosopher. He was only concerned with practically mitigating the phenomena of suffering, not in philosophical speculations about it. He said that feeling the experience wisely is enough to learn how to relieve it.

While we continue to explore what consciousness is, defining it and its mechanisms remains a mystery.

Implications for Meditation

Let's consider some of the implications this has for how we meditate. Pleasure and pain can give birth to desire. The traditional, moralistic view of desire is that it is bad because it is greedy, hateful, and/or deluded. The homeostatic view is that desire can be a source of wisdom. Yes, it can get distorted. But until we see the wisdom and compassion within desire, we have missed something essential.

If desire arises in meditation, it sometimes helps to take it at face value. If, for example, our mind is fuzzy and tired, one option is to take a nap. If we're hungry, perhaps our blood sugar is low. Eating a piece of fruit may bring balance. If we're antsy, the body might need more exercise.

As we've seen, complex organisms have lots of homeostatic processes, and sometimes homeostatic variables clash. Our system brings them into consciousness as emotions because our blind instincts need some help. So, taking them at face value might help. If we aren't sure, we can do an empirical trial: try it and see what happens.

If the mind-heart does not quiet or if another similar desire pops up, then we may need a different strategy, such as letting awareness broaden. Buddhism suggests that when awareness is wide, deep, and clear enough, we will naturally know what to do and what not to do. Thus we let the awareness be less like a cup of water and more like the Ganges River (p. 35).

For example, rather than just being aware of the object of desire, we include its feeling tone. Rather than limiting attention to a nap, food, or exercise, we turn toward and relax into the feeling of fatigue, hunger, or antsy-ness.

In this way we avail ourselves of the possibility that the desire may be wise but has the wrong focus. It may have latched onto the wrong object. The object of desire does not always come first and then generate the desire. More often, the desire arises first and looks around for what may be easy to see. But what's easy to see may not be the true cause. The reason awareness misses the mark can be our personal history, psychological dynamics, conditioning, or other factors. We don't have to analyze the situation. We just widen the field of awareness and look more openly at what's going on.

Here's an example: while I was supposedly meditating, I was worrying about an upcoming meeting that might be difficult. I'd already thought through various contingencies, so there was nothing more I could do about it at that moment. So I shifted my attention from the object of my fretfulness (all those meeting scenarios I kept rehearsing) to the process of thinking and its qualities: how was the mind feeling? Fast or slow? Light or heavy? Clear or opaque? Wide open or tightly focused? Quiet or chatty? I ignored the content and relaxed into the emotional tone itself.

The mind-heart is more sensitive when it's in "receiving mode" than when it's in "problem-solving mode." With that sensitivity I noticed a low-grade panic within the worry. In affective emotions, panic and grief often arise out of a sense of separation or loss of CONNECTION. So I relaxed and opened up a little more. Sure enough, there was a touch of loneliness — I felt alienated from the meeting environment I was anticipating.

So I turned toward and relaxed into that loneliness. As I felt it more directly, I didn't feel quite so alienated. It was as if I was no longer alone because the feeling had my attention.

It started to relax and spread out. It softened and gradually drifted away. Serenity and contentment seeped in. Soon the coming meeting did not feel like a big deal and the current moment felt peaceful.

I was aided in this inquiry by my knowledge of the affective emotions and knowing the cluster of separation, panic, and grief that often arise together. But I didn't create the loneliness. I just recognized the feeling sitting there quietly.

Wisdom Within Desire

There's another way to explore desire meditatively without knowing anything about affective emotions. It's the radical acceptance we visited in Chapter 3 (pp. 44-46). It starts from the premise that desires are not beasts or demons but rather, if we relate to them skillfully, entry points into deeper wellbeing. We treat desire as a messenger or guide to talk with like a friend: "If I could satisfy that desire, what would that give me?" And "If I had whatever it gave me, what would that give me in turn?" And so on.

For example, let's say I want a new cell phone. Rather than focusing on a phone, I explore the desire. An inner dialogue might look like this:

Question: If I were to get a new cell phone, what would that give me?

Answer: It would be more convenient.

Q: What would convenience give me?

A: My life would be a little easier.

Q: If my life were easier, what would that give me?

A: I'd be more content.

Q: If I were more content, what would that give me?

A: More contentment.

Repeating this kind of question is like asking, "What is it I really want behind everything?" Many desires are stand-in symbols for something deeper. When we follow those inward, we eventually come to the core desire. We know this because the answer to the question repeats itself.

At this point, the exercise shifts. We turn toward and relax into that deeper desire. With core desires, the resolution is often found within the desire itself. It points to something "in here" rather than "out there."

In this case, the core desire was contentment. The funny thing about contentment is that it is with us all the time, but we may be too busy or distracted to notice. So if we relax into the yearning for contentment, we may notice that it is here already, quietly waiting to be felt.

Attunement, Not Attainment

You can test this out. Look deep inside and see if behind all those thoughts there's a quiet place. It doesn't jump up and down and yell for attention. It is patient and quiet. If we just turn toward and relax into any moment, we may begin to see it and feel it. Our deepest yearnings often have what we yearn for hidden within them.

That source of peace and contentment is not something we create so much as it is something we discover again and again and again. It is not about attainment, but attunement.[22]

[22] For some people this attunement can be accompanied by subtle physiological changes, such as a quiet dropping sensation. These are the markers of clear awareness as described in Chapter 6 (p. 71).

If we treat desires as messengers rather than as problems, then the issue is how to listen more deeply to what's beyond the sometimes-superficial presentation.

You can probably come up with some variations on this exercise. One is to ask at any place in the chain of questions, "Whatever the deeper yearning is, what is another way to satisfy that?" Another variation is to ask any urge, "What do I really want?" as you turn toward it and relax more deeply.

None of this precludes my getting another cell phone. That may be practical. But if I want to lead a more fulfilling life, it is wise to use desires to see if there is something less superficial below it that is trying to be known.

On or off the meditation cushion, this is a way to treat our homeostatic imbalances as friends and guides to enriched living.

Nondual

One last note on desire.

As mentioned before, our brains have around 86 billion neurons. Neurons average about 7,000 synaptic connections to other neurons. Our neural networks are vast with many, many circuits and subcircuits within them. More than one circuit is likely to be active at any given time, so there is nothing to preclude our having opposing thoughts and feelings simultaneously.

I refer to this as "nondual awareness" (p. 75). There are many different philosophical descriptions of nondualism in which things that seem dichotomous (such as mind and body or seer and seen) appear to be distinct while not actually being separate. "Nondual awareness" refers desires, urges, feelings, sensations, or states which may seem in conflict with each other. Yet, in fact, many of them can be present at the same time. Contentment and discontent, pleasure and pain, comfort and discomfort, constriction and boundlessness, feeling fragmented and feeling whole can be with us all at once. And when we see them this way, they seem much less personal.

When these arise spontaneously, we can turn toward and relax into all these states at the same time even if they diverge. We simply let them all be there at once.

As Ralph Waldo Emerson put it in his 1841 essay "Self-Reliance": "A foolish consistency is the hobgoblin of little minds, adored by little statesmen and philosophers and divines. With consistency a great soul has simply nothing to do."

Empirical Trials

By shifting our language and thinking from "greed, hatred, and delusion" to "homeostasis," we can begin to see the imbalances that arise naturally in the mind-heart as just that: natural processes. It's futile to try to get rid of them, because they are built into the neural network. We cannot avoid them. And they are not personal. But we have a wide range of options as to how to relate to them. With fierce openness and acceptance, homeostatic imbalances resolve themselves and draw forth wisdom and insights.

To do this it often helps to play with them in a light way — to conduct verbal empirical trials that are not meant to confirm a philosophical stance but to just see more deeply and clearly what is true. We can try on different labels like "imbalance," "exaggeration," or "point of view" and see if it rings truer.

Fighting reality is a losing battle. But reality is our friend if we see it lucidly, without giving it a hard time for being what it is.

We'll come back to homeostasis on a subtler level in Chapter 13 (pp. 181-183) when we explore untangling the self. But in order to lay the groundwork for that, it would be helpful to look at a few other topics that have been raised so far.

I've talked about knowing what's going on out there or in here as if it's merely a matter of perception. But it's more bizarre and complicated than looking out the window or taking our pulse. We take little snippets of data and construct a model of reality. And the way we construct reality often has more influence than the data we receive at a given moment. We *infer* reality as much as we perceive it.

That is the topic of the next chapter.

Constructing a World

9

Guessing Reality: The Brain as a Modeling Machine

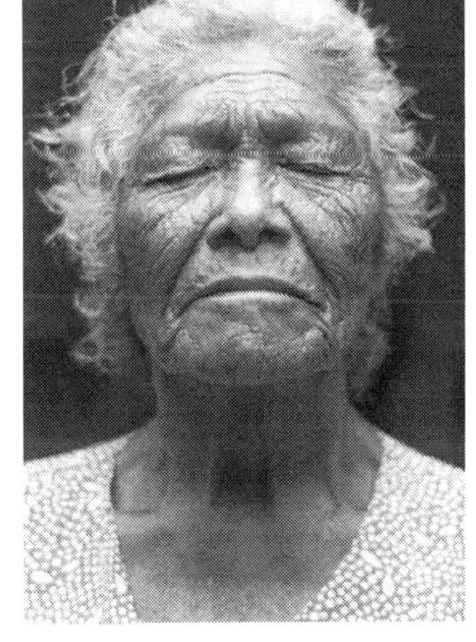

It's dark up there inside our skull. Light can't penetrate the dense, bony enclosure. There are no smells, no tastes, no tactile sensations. Sound waves may get through if they are loud enough. But the brain itself has no sound receptors. The ears are embedded in the side of the skull where they send neural signals inward along the auditory nerve.

The only information that gets directly to the brain are neural impulses. The human brain's 86 billion neurons constitute only 2 percent of the body's mass, yet they consume about 20 percent of its energy. If it processed every signal sent its way, the brain would be overwhelmed by the neural bombardment. Fortunately, many of the signals are redundant and can be safely ignored. Other signals get there highly processed.

For example, light travels through the lens of the eye, where it is turned upside down before striking the rods and cones in the retina at the back of the eye. The retina only responds to a small range of light waves — waves shorter than infrared and longer than ultraviolet. These are the most likely frequencies to come from a yellow star like our sun. Only this small range of colors fires neural impulses.

Some ganglia at the back of the retina respond only to contrasts — lines and edges. That is why it's easier to focus on the edge of an object than on a blank wall. The eyes shift more quickly when we are looking at a uniform surface because the redundant information is mostly filtered out and doesn't hold the eye's attention.

These massaged signals are passed through the nervous system to the visual centers in the brain. As they travel, they are further consolidated into shapes, objects, and scenes.

Even if a shape is complex, if it is familiar to the brain, it is redundant and not passed along farther. In this way, the brain doesn't waste energy in processing what it already knows.

All the sensory systems work this way: consolidating and filtering out information they don't need. For example, familiar sounds drift into the background while unexpected sounds grab our attention. People who live in cities don't hear many of the sounds around them that carry little useful information. However, if such city dwellers visit a quiet wilderness setting, the relative silence may feel odd until they get used to it. They may feel uneasy with the stillness until they get acclimated.

By not processing already familiar stimuli, an organism conserves energy for other things and thereby increases its chances of surviving, reproducing, and passing on its genes.

Markov Blanket

In Chapter 7 (pp. 94-95) we noted that for an organism to exist, it must have a boundary that separates it from its environment, otherwise it would be indistinguishable from the world, like a drop of ink in a glass of water. Part of our boundary is our skin. Part of a fish's boundary is its scales. Part of a tree's boundary is its bark.

To be considered alive (pp. 95-99), an organism must also do something to maintain its boundaries. It has to sense its world and manipulate it to some degree. Activity requires energy. So it must also extract energy resources (i.e., food). There are many ways to do that. We humans use sensory organs (eyes, ears, noses, etc.) to sense our surroundings and action organs (muscles and bones) to move our hands, feet, and so on. A tree draws air and sunlight in through its leaves and water and nutrients through its roots. It moves its leaves to face the sun by differential growth along its stems and limbs. It moves its roots by sensing water and nutrients and then growing in those directions.

In these ways, a living organism is separate from its environment and, at the same time, interacts with it.

Mathematically, this separate but interactional capability is called a Markov blanket.[23] The "blanket" has a sensory layer and a motor layer. The sensory layer picks up information from the world, codes it, and transmits it to the inner organism (the brain). The motor layer picks up directions from the brain and sends them to the muscles in order to manipulate the outside world.

When I first heard of a Markov blanket, I found the term confusing. For touch sensation, it makes sense to call it a blanket since the skin covers the body like a blanket. But for sights and sounds, the term sounds odd. But it's just a

---

[23] Andrey Andreyevich Markov (June 14, 1856 – July 20 1922) was a Russian mathematician best known for his work on models of sequences of possible events in which the probability of each event depends on the previous events.

metaphor and is not to be taken literally. For sight, the sensory layer is physically very small: the lens and retina which transduce light into neural impulses. For sounds, the Markov sensory layer includes the ear structures that pick up sound waves and transduce them into nerve impulses.

And though it is a metaphor, there are very real neural circuits that connect the motor and sensory functions that play a role in the sense of self, as we'll see in Chapter 10.

In this way, the brain and the outside world are never in direct contact with each other but do pass coded messages back and forth through the organism's Markov blanket. They are separate yet they interact.

By the way, we have more than the five senses mentioned by Aristotle: seeing, hearing, tasting, smelling, and touch. Other senses that neural scientists generally agree on include thermoception (sense of heat), nociception (perception of pain), equilibrioception (perception of balance), and proprioception (nonvisual body awareness as illustrated by closing your eyes and touching your nose). Some scientists say we have twenty-one or up to fifty-three senses. They all have their own Markov blankets.

Modeling Machine

Since the brain receives the signals from a vast array of neurons and hormones and no other information, it must weave those signals together into a model of what's out there. It does this so convincingly that we assume our model of the world is real, solid, tangible, and exactly what the brain constructs. It does this with such a smooth sleight of hand that we are hoodwinked into believing the world is exactly as we imagine.

Yet in reality, the brain is a modeling machine, constantly guessing what's out there. Its guesses are not a total fabrication because it keeps sampling the incoming sensory, neural, and hormonal signals to see if its model is holding up. The neural scientist Anil Seth calls this a "controlled hallucination." It's a "hallucination" because we construct our sense of the world rather than perceiving it directly. And it's "controlled" because we constantly check the model for accuracy. When the incoming signals clash with our constructed reality, these "error corrections" are used to update our model of the world — update the hallucination, if you will.

We'll get to how we process these updates and error corrections in the next chapter. But for now I want to emphasize that the brain actively guesses and from those guesses constructs a model of reality rather than passively perceiving it.

This makes a lot of sense to me in the abstract. But when I look inside, I don't see a model. Quite the opposite. As I walk through the woodlands and fields, the belief that I'm seeing the real world is quite compelling. The ground seems to slip by beneath me. I see tiny purple flowers in tufts of grass, pieces of broken leaves, small beetles, a Black Phoebe watching me from a sycamore. None of this seems like a model or a hallucination.

Of course, from the perspective of evolution, there is no survival advantage in seeing the model as a model. Accuracy is less important than effectiveness. Believing the model is real is effective even if that is not totally accurate.

But still, I wasn't convinced. I wanted to know the model itself. What did it feel like? How did it manifest? I couldn't see it directly. Then I stubbed my toe and suddenly it became crystal clear.

Stubbed Toe

As I walked past a table in the family room, my foot strayed to the side and collided with the table leg. A bright image flashed in my mind of the two smallest toes spread apart by the table leg. My shoulders reflexively dropped as I stooped over to take some weight off that foot. Words flashed through my mind: "This is going to hurt." The words weren't "This hurts." Rather they were a guess that it would hurt.

And sure enough, a moment later searing pain rose through me. I let out a colorful expletive (as if that might relieve some of the burning sensation). This was followed by a thought, "This will pass. Just hang in for a few minutes."

So I hung in. In a few minutes the feeling was tolerable. I checked to see if my toes were dislocated — they weren't. But I knew I'd be limping for the next ten or fifteen minutes.

As my system wound down out of emergency mode, I remembered how I'd been trying to understand how we construct models of the world. How did I know my toes would hurt fiercely in a few seconds? How did I know that the pain would subside in ten or fifteen minutes?

The obvious answer was I knew these things from experience — I have stubbed my toes a few times a year for years. Each time there is that curious time gap between knowing I have kicked something and the arrival of the pain. Each time the pain has subsided in five to fifteen minutes.

I was curious about the time delay and eventually learned how that worked. We have two nervous systems that register sights, sounds, and touch. The first system registers pain. Its neurons do not have myelin sheathing, which makes them relatively slow. They send signals to the ventral or lower parts of the brain. The second system came later in evolution. It registers location. Its neurons have myelin sheathing making them relatively fast. They send signals to the dorsal part of the brain across the top of the head.

The fast touch signals tell me where the signal is coming from and the slower pain signals tell me how it feels.

When sensations are triggered in the upper body — say, a pinch on the ear — the difference between how long it takes the two kinds of neural signals to reach the brain is relatively trivial. I hardly notice a time lag.

But the toes and the brain are far apart with a long neural pathway between them. So the fast touch signals reach the brain a few seconds ahead of the slow pain signals.

So when I stubbed my toe again, the mind predicted the aftermath would unfold in the same way as it had in the past. I could not see a model or diagram of this in my head. But I predicted pain would arise in a few seconds and subside in ten or fifteen minutes because this is what happened so many times before. If I hadn't known anatomy, I might have come up with a different explanation — perhaps that demons were punishing me for being clumsy.

Anticipation and Expectancy

However, in the moment of stubbing my toe, what I felt was anticipation. Anticipation might imply a model of myself and the world, but the moment-to-moment experience was expectancy.

When I look at life around me, I can see that I have lots of expectations: the sun will rise in the east; my cat would like to sleep under the covers on cold nights; my grandson wants a bedtime story; there will be bananas in the grocery store in aisle 3. I can abstract those expectancies into a model of the world and myself. But they first surface as predictions.

The Other Outdoors

I, of course, am not alone in making predictions or creating models. They are woven into our lives and into the lives of the creatures around us.

I can even see them in my cats. They seem to construct reality in their minds, but it takes them longer and they make more mistakes because they have a smaller neocortex. For example, they like being outside, but not when it's raining. When it starts to sprinkle, they call out to be let in the front door. As soon as they get inside, they go to the back door and meow to be let out. As my wife surmises, "They want the *other* outdoors." Their model of the world has not yet put together that if it's raining in the front outdoors, it will probably be raining in the back outdoors too.

But eventually they learn.

Consolidation

When we encounter a new event, the brain predicts what it thinks will happen. If the incoming signal from the unfolding event matches expectations at any stage along the path from sensory organ to the processing center in the brain, the incoming signals are dropped. Its expectation has been corroborated, so there is no need to process it any further. But if the signal is not what it predicted, then a potential error has been detected. The neural signals are sent on up the line and continue to be processed.

This may seem like a lot of fuss over a simple experience. But it turns out that this "fuss" saves energy. There is enough redundancy that spending a little energy to filter out unnecessary information is more efficient than processing everything.

By the way, this model of what the brain expects is part of the beginning of a sense of self. We'll come back to it in Chapter 11.

Who's That?

Even if you don't stub your toes a few times each year, you can still verify modeling and filtering in other experiences if you pay careful attention. For example, Bob said he was coming over to see me. I knew he drove a small blue car.

Glancing out my window, I saw a small blue car stopping in front of my house. If Bob had stepped out, there would have been no need to process it any further. My system would not have put any effort into planning my next move because everything was going according to the existing plan.

But instead, a woman stepped out of the car. I was surprised. My energy perked up: "Who's that?" I looked more intently and recognized my next-door neighbor. Then my system relaxed.

This is an example of the affective emotion SEEKING getting triggered. You may remember that when something strange or unexpected shows up in the world around us, this SEEKING emotion gets activated (pp. 16-18). It pushes us to figure things out.

This was a minor situation and only a small amount of extra energy was needed. But it illustrates how, throughout the day, when things meet our predictions, we save precious resources by unconsciously reverting to the model of what was supposed to happen.

Mirror on the Wall

Of course, failing to process some things can result in errors.

There was a mirror hanging over the wall of my dresser. When our one-year-old granddaughter came for a visit, we used that dresser for a changing table. When she was being diapered, she liked to grab or kick the mirror. So my wife replaced the mirror with a familiar painting whose bottom edge was out of her reach.

Problem solved.

Several days after the visit, I was putting on a T-shirt in front of the dresser. I looked down as I pulled it over my head and thought I noticed a smudge. I immediately looked into the mirror for a better look at my shirt.

But the mirror wasn't there. It was now in the closet, while the painting was hanging on the wall.

I had only vaguely noticed when the mirror had been replaced with a familiar painting. It requires some energy to update my models of the world. Instinctively it had not felt important enough to update my internal model of the dresser. At least it was not important until I needed the mirror again.

Stories

Prediction, expectation, anticipation — what these have in common is that they are a short series of events in which one incident leads to another. A long series of events is a story. We humans love series and we love stories.

We tell our children stories in the evening to help them feel cared for and fall asleep. We read novels, watch movies, and check the latest news reports. If I, as a writer, want you to remember a particular point, I know that if I illustrate the point with a story, there is a much greater chance that in three months you will remember the story and its point than if I just tell you the point without a story.

We also use stories to knit ourselves together into families, tribes, and nations. Stories can impart a sense of meaning and purpose.

When a sequence of actions or a story is repeated over and over, it can solidify into a model of reality. As we noted earlier, the brain uses a relatively large amount of the body's energy. So anything that can reduce the energy it needs can be beneficial. Key aspects of a story get abstracted from a sequence of movements into a simplified static picture of the world. This model, in turn, filters how we perceive events. It helps consolidate our thinking and saves precious energy.

Top Down

In this way, perception is mostly driven from the top down rather than from the bottom up. We may think that perception is driven only from the sense data — the little bits of information that stream in from the sense organs and flow up to the brain, where they are assembled into a model of reality.

It is disheartening to see how easy it is for progressives and conservatives to look at the same political landscape and draw radically different conclusions. Each is baffled that the other sees things so differently. We presume that we are looking at the same world. But the problem is we aren't looking through the same minds. The brain and its models have a huge influence over what we consider important and what can be ignored — even if it's as big as a ship.

If we don't like the way a person is treating us, we may simplify the story into a model that declares either "He's bad" or "I'm bad." When Vladimir Putin wanted Ukraine to be part of his Russia, this solidified into a simple idea that Ukraine was not really a separate country. He used selective history to justify his model.

One of the things that makes it hard to bridge our differences is that our models of reality are difficult to see as *models* rather than as *reality*. Models are like the Wizard of Oz hiding behind a curtain as he secretly pulls levers and controls. We need a Toto to pull the curtain back and expose the inner workings.

The Buddhist equivalent of Toto is clear awareness. Clear awareness pulls back the curtain by dropping all its assumptions and looking with quiet receptivity — Suzuki Roshi famously called this "beginner's mind." We look afresh with few assumptions.

The old saying goes, "I'll believe it when I see it." The truth is usually the opposite: "I'll see it when I believe it."

The situation is not hopeless. There is a stream of data that flows in. If we understand that perceptions can be distorted by hidden models, it is a little easier to drop our assumptions and see, hear, and think with fresh minds. This allows us to update our models more easily. But the first step is to understand that we all have models and we can't escape from being affected by them. Once we realize that, we can step back and look anew.

Unconscious Actions

Actions start from a lot of physical motions we don't think about after we have learned them.

If I want a sandwich from the refrigerator, most of my actions are automated. I don't think about how to move my feet to get to the refrigerator. I don't think about which muscles I'll need to use to activate my hand and fingers to grab the refrigerator door. I don't think about which muscles to activate to look around inside the refrigerator to find the sandwich. Mostly I'm thinking about whether I want to add mustard and a pickle or just eat it as is.

All those so-called voluntary actions are done without conscious attention because the brain has built a smoothly working series of actions that need to be taken to get the sandwich. At most I think, "I'll look in the refrigerator," whereupon those learned patterns know what to do without conscious attention. I was not born with those muscle patterns ready to go. I learned them over the years through trial and error and practice.

If you like, try this now: Open your hand, make a fist, then relax it.

Notice you probably didn't think about each muscle involved. You have a schema in your brain that will fire them in the right sequence when you think, "Make a fist." The details handle themselves.

We are born knowing how to perform only a few essential movements, such as how to turn our head and to nurse. An infant can't even hold a rattle or put her thumb in her mouth without risking poking herself in the eye.

The mind is a predicting-modeling machine that learns from experience the same way I learned my toe would hurt a few seconds after kicking the table.

What I'm describing now are the so-called voluntary muscle systems, which we can control a little at a time with volition and training.

The majority of what our bodies do is ordinarily beyond the reach of volition. The body moves blood through veins and arteries, decides when and how to digest food, opens and closes pores on the skin in response to temperature changes, detects invading microorganisms and manufactures specific antibodies, carries dead cells out of the system and grows new ones, processes sensory signals, raises and lowers blood pressure, and on and on. We don't have conscious diagrams of all this and no direct way to control thousands of essential things our body must do to stay alive.

And if we had to track and tend to all those things with deliberate awareness, we'd be overwhelmed by the details.

When Predictions Fail

After we have built up these automated patterns and models, we aren't done. It is important to update them as life around us changes. The more adaptable we are, the more likely we will pass our genes on. When the incoming signals do not match our existing expectations, we can throw out the old model and build a new one (which I did when Bob didn't step out of the blue car — see p. 129). Or we can throw out the data and stick with the old model (which I did with the mirror over my dresser until that stopped working — see pp. 129-130).

There is a third option. In complex situations, it takes the least amount of energy to accept what turned out as expected and, at the same time, update the model to incorporate the new information. This is called "Bayesian inference." It is more complicated, yet very important. We'll look at it in the next chapter.

But before we do that, let's pause for a moment and look at the implications modeling and anticipation have for meditation practice.

Implications for Meditation

Intending, expecting, anticipating, and modeling are actions in the present that look to the future. The processes are happening now. The anticipated outcomes are projections forward in time.

Meditation works, in part, by attending to the present. But the mind is not "bad" for anticipating the future. It is an evolutionary mechanism that helps keep us alive. It is deeply wired into us when we feel any kind of threat.

So don't try to discard these predictions out of hand. If there's something to them — you forgot to turn off the stove, the window is open and it's raining, etc. — by all means take care of business.

But there are many false alarms. There may be nothing that needs our attention right now. In that case, we can reassure the mind-heart that we're okay and bring awareness back to the present by shifting attention from the thoughts about the future to the present processes of anticipating or imagining — how does the mind-heart feel as it does that? We can turn toward and relax into any tension we notice (Chapter 5, Ennobling Practices, pp. 59-66).

Also, as meditative awareness gets subtler and more sensitive, we may get flashes of things that are not so nice and may not be about the future. Why would we push something out of awareness in the first place? It is probably not because it felt great or was something we felt proud of. Probably the opposite.

So growing awareness can be one insult after another as old hurts, mean-spiritedness, and fears that were once nicely hidden get their covers blown. Again, if there is any charge in these images and memories, we turn toward the charge, relax into it, and savor/smile.

But as awareness deepens, there may be little flashes that have very little charge — images that come and go quickly. We can just let them go through. They're remnants of old stuff that was mostly but not completely worked out. If there's more to them, they'll come back again — we can be sure of that. Some of them may seem strange, as if they are leftovers from a dream or another life. They can also be precursors (*saṅkhāra* or formations) that don't have much content at all. We just observe them without holding on or pushing away; rather, we let them go on their way.

By letting awareness be receptive without trying to search for something that is not apparent, we treat these flashes as if they are not us. And they aren't! They're just a passing parade. No need to engage.

10

Updating Reality: Top-Down Bayesian Inference

As we saw in the last chapter, the mind creates models of reality and uses those models to guide behavior. But what happens when the models are off the mark? The world is complicated and so are we, so it's inevitable that our models are guesses or inferences at best. What do we do when we realize we got it wrong?

One option is to throw out the model and start over. But if the model is only a little off, starting over can be unnecessarily burdensome in terms of time and energy. The other option is to upgrade our models. This, too, can be complicated. But it turns out in the long run that updating is much more efficient.

This upgrading is called Bayesian inference after Charles Bayes, a Presbyterian minister, philosopher, and statistician in eighteenth-century England. He worked out the mathematical formulas through which existing models can be tweaked and upgraded by incorporating small amounts of new information. His math also considers the reliability of the information — how confident we are in it. The math is complex. But it works surprisingly well in describing how our brains work.

Rather than go through all the math, it might be more informative to tell a story that illustrates what this looks like in real life.

Scratches in the Night

I woke up to a soft scratching in the middle of the night. What was it? The bedroom window was open. The sounds seemed to be coming from the roof.

The bird feeder outside attracts lots of songbirds: sparrows, towhees, titmice, phoebes, and more. It was easy to imagine the sounds coming from bird feet in the metal gutters.

This is an example of abductive reasoning. Most people are familiar with deductive reasoning: all cats are mortal, Lila is a cat, therefore Lila is mortal. If the facts are true and the logic is sound, we are guaranteed to get a true answer.

Abductive reasoning is looser. Our observations are incomplete, so the best we can do is to make a prediction: all cats are mortal, Lila is mortal, therefore Lila is a cat. Abductive inferences are not always true. Lila could be a hamster and the first two statements would still be true.

Inferences are best guesses based on incomplete information. In our lives, we rarely have all the information. If we waited to do something until we reached certainty, we would often be waiting a long time.

I knew a lot of songbirds came through our yard, so when I heard the scratches in the night, it was a reasonable guess that the sounds were coming from them. But there were other possibilities, too. This is the nature of abductive reasoning.

The next night I was awakened again. This time the scratches were accompanied by soft rustling. I also noticed that there were no bird songs or chirping. It was the middle of the night, after all, when songbirds often snooze. So it was less likely that the sounds came from bird feet. Perhaps squirrels were scampering through the gutters.

I went to the window and listened more carefully, the scratching could have been coming from the roof or the attic or inside the wall. It was less likely that a bird would crawl into the attic. A small mammal was more inclined. I didn't like the thought of smelly critters up there.

Now we are in the realm of Bayesian inference. It is abductive reasoning with a few additional factors thrown in: new information and estimates of the reliability of existing information.

As before, my observations were incomplete: none of my clues were ironclad. But I did have more evidence to add to my previous observations: no singing, only rustling sounds, ambiguity as to where the murmurs were coming from, etc.

One of the hallmarks of Bayesian inference is that over time we may get new information that changes our predictions. Also, with new information our confidence in the old information may drift.

The next day I got a ladder out and inspected the roof and gutters. There was a place where the planes of the roof came together leaving a big hole up under an eave. I had not known about that. It was well sheltered by the overhang so no rain could get in without flowing uphill. But little critters? They can walk uphill. Even Lila goes up on the roof at times and would be able to find her way from the roof directly into the attic.

In fact, the hole was large enough for a raccoon to fit through. I had never seen raccoons in the neighborhood. But they are nocturnal creatures and could be around without being seen. And there are squirrels — we see lots of them. I have not seen rats, but we live near a river, which rats like. And they can be very quiet and nocturnal. So there were many possibilities: rats, cat, squirrels, raccoons, birds, and probably a few more I hadn't thought of. Squirrels seemed the most likely culprits.

Over the next few days I got some hardware cloth and blocked the hole under the eaves. That would keep out squirrels, birds, raccoons, and Lila.

All was quiet for the next few nights. Hooray!

Bayesian inference is based on more than a momentary assessment at one point in time. It is dynamic and can change over minutes, hours, days, and even years. In the intervening time we can and often do seek more information, which can change the Bayesian calculations.

My investigation of the roof yielded new information and shed new light on the salience of old information. The big hole increased the likelihood of a large intruder, though it didn't rule out the little guys. If it was a large animal, blocking the hole could stop it from getting in. In fact, that did seem to solve the problem.

The scientific method is an example of Bayesian inference. We have hypotheses — guesses based on limited information — and we experiment to test those hypotheses. If we're good scientists, we use our results to refine our theories.

Notice that none of this proved it had been a large animal. But it shifted the odds in that direction until …

Several days later, the sounds returned: scratching, rustling, and even something that sounded like gnawing. And it continued on and off throughout the night.

So much for my squirrel theory. There was no way a creature that size could get in now that the big hole was secured. Rats now went to the top of my list of likely intruders.

The next day I got up on the ladder again and checked the house from rooftop to foundation for tiny openings. Rats can squeeze through very small apertures. I used steel wool to plug about a half dozen cracks where they might breach my defenses.

It worked! For the next few months there were only the sounds of crickets, cicadas, and the breeze coming from outside. And birdsongs near dawn, but not from the roof or the attic. There was no more scratching or rustling in the wee hours of the night.

Three months later the sounds were back. Ahh!

Plugging even the smallest holes should theoretically have stopped the rats from getting in. But most scientific theories are proven wrong in time. Maybe not completely wrong, but not completely right either. In science this is called "verisimilitude" — finding answers that are more and more true, but not flawless.

The same is true with Bayesian inference — verisimilitude means that our guesses are better but may not be completely correct.

I considered putting rat traps in the attic. But I don't like to kill creatures just because they are inconvenient for me. After all, their ancestors were living on this land for hundreds or thousands of years before white settlers erected their boxy abodes. We had invaded their land rather than them invading ours. And they were just trying to live out their lives — just as all creatures try to do.

I wanted to find a way we could peacefully coexist.

Still, they might gnaw attic wires and touch off a fire. That may be unlikely, but if they did, the results would be catastrophic for both them and me. It was worrisome.

I got out my ladder again to inspect the perimeter. This time I recognized a hole in the defenses that I had overlooked before. We had an exhaust fan over the kitchen stove. The vent ran up the wall between the kitchen and a bedroom and then poked up through the roof. A big piece of curved metal covered the vent like an umbrella. It kept the rain out. But it left another opening where an acrobatic rat or even a squirrel might find entry.

I got out my hardware cloth and put a mesh over the opening.

Nocturnal bliss resulted. For the next six months there was not a sound. I was sure my nemeses had been small rodents and that I'd finally constructed an impenetrable perimeter. We could now live in peace together. I didn't mind them running over the roof or around the yard so long as I could fence them out of the house.

As Robert Frost wrote: "Good fences make good neighbors."

Epilogue:

Eight months later I was awakened by the familiar sounds of rustling, gnawing, and scratching. And they seemed to be coming from inside the wall. I felt disheartened. I was sure they were back in the attic but had no idea how they got in.

However, after about twenty minutes, the sounds stopped and it was quiet for the rest of the night.

The next morning I inspected the vent on the roof. All my fortifications were secure.

As I thought it through, I realized the critters may not have actually gotten in this time. If a rat had been on the roof scratching to get in the vent, the sounds would have easily traveled down the sheet metal pipe from the outside. If a persistent rat had scratched and prodded on the roof for twenty minutes, the scratching sound could have traveled far. Maybe the rat had tried to get in but failed to breach the perimeter.

This hypothesis fit the evidence snuggly.

Ever since, the nights have been quiet up there except for about twenty minutes every three or four months. I imagine a new rat sniffing the warmth from the exhaust vent and trying to break in. Fortunately it fails and moves on.

I can be at peace with them prodding

several times a year. So long as I can keep them out of my inner sanctum, I am content.

And I hope the rats are too.

Good fences can make good neighbors.

Brain in the Dark

This is an example of Bayesian inference. We gather bits of inconclusive data and make best guesses as to what created that information. It's rarely conclusive. We may gather more data either passively or actively. We use the new results to update our guesses. And we repeat this process as often as we're interested and able.

With this in mind, let's go back to the brain sitting up there inside the dark enclosure of the skull. It's isolated from direct contact with the world by its various Markov blankets (pp. 119-124). The only hints it has about the outside world are little neural blips.

In my story, the most relevant blips were auditory signals. I tried several times to get visual confirmation by sneaking out in the dark with a flashlight to see the critters that were doing the scratching and gnawing. But their auditory acuity was greater than mine. The scratching always stopped before I could get out the door. I never actually saw them.

The only data I had were those neural potentials flowing down neural axons from my ears to the neural web of my brain. That network constructed models of what was going on. It guessed, adjusted, collected more information, and guessed again. This is all the brain can ever do.

It's not surprising that its guesses are sometime off. It's amazing that the system works as often as it does!

It took millions of years of evolutionary trial and error to evolve these capacities. We make a vast number of Bayesian inferences every day. Fortunately, most of the calculations happen without our conscious intervention — they are below the level of awareness. If we had to give conscious attention to each of them, we'd be overwhelmed by all the processing. Consider: I sit here typing words on a keyboard without thinking about the keys I press. At the same time my stomach digests food without explicit instructions from me. I sip from a water bottle on my desk while my mind's attention is on the meaning of this paragraph. Most of this is outside conscious knowing.

And yet, I get by just fine most of the time. As do we all.

Top-Down Perception

Bayesian inference implies that perception is "top-down" rather than "bottom-up." The bottom-up model says that there is an objective reality out there and we are neutral observers who simply take in information (sights, sounds, touch sensations, etc.). As the information flows up from the sensory organs through the nervous system and brain, it is processed and assembled into objects and scenes.

This model seems intuitively obvious. Yet it also seems intuitively obvious that the sun revolves around the earth. But we all know that's an illusion.

The top-down model of perception says the brain would have trouble processing anything if it didn't know what to expect. So perception is more like hypothesis testing. The brain is constantly making predictions about the causes of sensory signals. These predictions flow from the top down through the brain and nervous system.

At the same time, sensory signals flow from the bottom up and check those predictions against the incoming data. If there is a mismatch or "prediction error," the brain adjusts its predictions so as to minimize the errors. Perception happens through an ongoing process of prediction-error minimization. We are not conscious to most of these prediction errors. All that we know directly are the predictions themselves. And they are constantly upgraded until they fit the data.

What's most important here is that *our felt experience comes from the brain's top-down predictions, not from the bottom-up signals.* Usually we don't notice the sensory signals as much as the top-down interpretations of them.

In this way, we can never be absolutely certain what is going on out there outside of our brains. But we can and do form hypotheses about the universe around us.

Error Corrections

Sometimes there is a large mismatch between the incoming data and our expectations. This kind of mismatch is uncomfortable. It creates a homeostatic imbalance that we're motivated to resolve. The motivator is called "pain" or "confusion."

There are lots of strategies for removing that discomfort and coming back into a more pleasurable homeostatic balance. One strategy is to get more information by simply attending more completely. The second night when the scratching sounds came back, I went to the window to listen from a different angle. I noticed the sounds may have been coming from the attic. That was more information. The next day, I climbed up a ladder to get even more information.

I used that information to update my understanding.

Inattentional Blindness

Another strategy for getting comfortable is to ignore the new information. Rather than attending more carefully, we ignore more diligently.

We actually do this more than we suspect, because when we do it well, we may not notice what we are doing. For example, a friend who was a kindergarten teacher was helping her students get ready to leave at the end of the day, when a little girl mumbled something softly. My friend was busy with other kids and didn't have enough spare attention to make out her student's soft words. She just said, "That's nice," and went on helping the kids get their jackets on.

Later that day, the little girl's mother called the teacher to say her daughter was upset that the teacher thought it was nice that her hamster had died.

This is called "inattentional blindness." We can only pay attention to a limited number of things, so sometimes we ignore some data.

There is a dramatic example of this in a film clip on YouTube from the lab of Daniel Simons. If you're interested, search for "Simons inattentional blindness," and take a look before reading further.

In the video you see two teams of six people. One team wears white shirts. The other wears black. They wander around randomly as they pass a basketball to their teammates. You are asked to count the number of passes made by the white team.

At the end of the film you're asked if you noticed anything unusual. Most people say no. Then you're asked if you noticed a man in a gorilla suit walking through and beating his chest. Most of them emphatically say no!

Then they replay the video. Now the gorilla is so obvious that many assume it is a different film. But it's not. One version of the film ends with the words "We only see what we attend to. Watch for bicyclists."

Context

Another implication of Bayesian inference is that when we perceive something, we are perceiving what is in the mind, not what is in the world. There are some red roses outside my window. But if the roses were white and it was night with a red light shining on them, they would appear red to me. The color of the light and the color of the flowers would blend together. The red is not in the flower, it is in the brain. The color is in my mind, not in the roses. And if I were colorblind, the roses might appear gray. There are complex factors that come together to make the color. The color is not out there in the world, it's in the brain and filtered through Bayesian inferences.

Illusions

Adelson Illusion

Optical illusions make the same point. In Edward H. Adelson's Checkerboard-Shadow Illusion, square A (second square in the top row) appears to be dark and square B (third square in the third row) appears to be light. In reality, both A and B are the same shade of gray. However, we automatically use Bayesian inference to shift our perception such that square B seems lighter because it's in the shadow of the cylinder. You can see this when we impose gray strips over both of the squares.

Adelson Illusion Explained

Because of how automated and effortless Bayesian inference is, it is still easier to "see" the A square as dark and the B square as light even when you know better.

In the old man and the dog illusion,[24] the context is a little subtler.

Face and Dog Illusion

It is the orientation of the drawing that confuses us. Turn it upside down and you can see a dog chewing a bone.

The old man and the dog are not on the page. They are in your brain. Depending on the orientation, we infer very different things for the shapes drawn on the page.

If I watch the drawings carefully as I slowly rotate the images 180 degrees, there is a moment about halfway around when I can see and feel the picture morph from a face to a dog or a dog to a face. The change seems to be on the page. But in reality, it's just in my mind. Because Bayesian inference is so deeply wired in and natural to us, it takes a lot more effort to keep seeing the man as a man or the dog as a dog as the image is rotated.

---

24 https://shareably.net/old-man-optical-illusion/

Implications for Meditation

Dog and Face Illusion

Too often meditators get ideas about how their mind or heart should be and try to emulate that. While the motives are admirable, the result is often that too much effort is spent trying to get our inner experience to line up with some predetermined ideal. As mentioned earlier, Shunryū Suzuki Roshi said, "In the beginner's mind there are many possibilities; in the expert's mind there are few."

The Buddha said that having a clear, unencumbered awareness supports inner freedom. He emphasized seeing reality as it is, not as we think it should be.

While I agree with Suzuki Roshi and the Buddha in many ways, it would be a mistake to take them too literally. The mind is never blank and its processes are never neutral. However, if we can see the brain's bias and our own personal leanings clearly enough, then we needn't be fooled by them.

As mentioned earlier, the brain comprises about 2 percent of our body weight but uses about 20 percent of the body's energy, thus it's to our benefit to use these resources economically. This is so helpful that over hundreds of thousands of years, energy-saving habits have been bred into us, including Bayesian inference. Bayesian inference evolved to operate behind the scenes. It saved energy and sped up processing time by automating decisions below the level of consciousness.

Newness requires more energy because we can't rely on old habits, including Bayesian inference. And it would take more energy to be present in the world if we were a blank slate. Even so-called beginner's mind comes with a lot of prewired circuits and previous experiences. Imagine having a new job, a new home, a new class, new friend, and a new child. We'd have to rearrange our schedules, find new stores, look up routes on maps, adjust to new personalities, and so on. Maybe the brain would consume 30 percent of our energy! It would be exhausting to get through the day until we had established some habits and routines that worked for us more or less automatically.

On the other hand, if we meditated in the same old way for a few years, it would probably bring the same old results. Advanced meditation practice is not one-size-fits-all. If we want to discover anything we don't know already, advanced practice requires adopting beginner's mind and looking afresh at what's going on.

If we want to see clearly, it helps to notice our assumptions and let them drop away as best we can: relax and open with few expectations. This includes seeing Bayesian inferences and checking to see if they really relate to our current situation or are just old habits that may have exhausted their usefulness.

This works in other areas of life as well. For example, it's easy to see how political opponents jump to unwarranted conclusions. It's hard to see the same tendencies in ourselves. This is because Bayesian inference quietly and effortlessly jumps to conclusions.

The remedy is paradoxical. We don't try to stop the leaps of mind. We try to observe them more mindfully. As we do that, we are less likely to be fooled by our own Bayesian leaps.

Here are a few strategies that can help:

Present

One strategy is to bring awareness as close to the present moment as we can — see what's actually here without assumptions about what's good or bad. As we get closer to the present, the mind gets simpler and less complicated.

We cannot do this completely. When we perceive something, it takes a moment for the brain to interpret it. So by the time we are conscious of it, it has already slipped into the immediate past.

However, if we bring awareness as close to the present as we can, thoughts about the past and the future tend to drop away. We see more of what is going on right now before anything is inferred.

Rather than quiet the mind, or substitute a practice for an old habit, we just see how close we can come to "now." With patience, the mind quiets itself.

Watch for Thoughts Arising

Another strategy is to watch thoughts arise and at the first hint of them, relax into them or use the Three Practices.

For us humans, thinking is an old survival strategy. We don't have big muscles, claws, or strong teeth. We just have big brains. When we're in a tight spot, rather than punch or claw or bite our way out, we try to figure our way out.

So when we're under stress, the mind tends to speed up. And conversely, when the mind speeds up, we feel stress. It works both ways: stress creates a speedy mind and a speedy mind creates stress. In both cases, it helps to see the speedy mind itself and relax into it. As the mind relaxes, it sees more clearly. And as we see more clearly, the mind relaxes.

Meanwhile, the mind gets more serene.

Less Technique, More Presence

All we can see from inside our skulls are the models we create and then update in order to infer what is out there. However, if we are more conscious of the modeling and updating processes, then we are better able to see all of this with fresh eyes rather than blind assumptions. As we get humbler about our perceptions, we get wiser.

It sounds simple. And it is. But it's not easy. There is more to meditation than getting technique just right. Technique may help in the beginning. But deeper meditation is about seeing / hearing / feeling / knowing things as they truly are, not how we model them behind our Markov blankets or adjust them using Bayesian inference. Our priority should be to focus less on technique and more on presence: on seeing the moment just as it is.

Observe "Error Corrections"

Another simple practice is to notice "error corrections" — discrepancies between what we expect and what actually happens — and watch for the tendency to discard things we don't like. Discarding is both natural and unhelpful. Better to see things as they are — no need to fix anything. Just observe what is.

Our sense of self and the nature of our consciousness are also influenced by Bayesian inferences. These are the topics we'll explore in the next several chapters.

Constructing a Self

11

Self as Process

The last Sunday in May 2004 was hot. But the evening was cool. I stood in our backyard gazing at the sky. The night was peaceful. I got a sleeping bag and pillow and stretched out on the patio lounge chair. I slept well.

In the morning, I got up, walked toward the back of the house, and reached for the doorknob.

The next thing I remember is seeing a blurry, gray strip across my field of vision. When I pulled my head back to see it more clearly, I recognized the strip as the rail of a hospital bed. Erika, my wife, was standing on one side. My son Nathan was on the other. "But he lives in Palo Alto — three hours away," I thought.

Outside my field of vision a strange voice asked, "What day is it?"

"I have no idea," I confessed.

"What year is it?"

"'Oh-four," I guessed.

"Good," the voice said.

I touched the top of my head. It was shaved clean except for some metal clamps. My ribs hurt as I raised my arm. I was vaguely aware of dull and sharp sensations all over my body.

"What's going on?" I wondered. An image popped into my mind of a pack of trolls. You know trolls: eight feet tall, stubby legs, large bodies, no necks, and persistent, mischievous grins. Obviously, marauding trolls had used me for a soccer ball.

I decided to get a second opinion. "What happened?" I asked Erika.

"You were in a bike accident." Her voice was kind and patient. Nathan had a similar benign smile. Later I learned that I had asked that same question every two or three minutes for the last six or eight hours. But until that moment, my brain had been incapable of retaining a memory.

It was four-thirty in the afternoon.

I was released from the hospital five days later. I still do not have any memory of what happened between reaching for the doorknob and guessing the year correctly. But the evidence suggests I went for a bike ride along the American River. Ten miles from home, the trail crosses a bridge and makes a sharp, steep turn. A sign says, "Walk. Do not ride bicycle." I, of course, rode the bike as I always do. But there was dry sand on the asphalt trail this time. The bike slipped and I lost control.

There is a four-foot fence between the trail and a thirty-foot drop into the river. I probably realized that if I hit the fence while sitting on the bike seat, I could flip over it and land on the rocks below. So I leaned back hard to bring the bike down and make sure my body hit the fence rather than catapulting over the top. As I fell, the back of my head hit the asphalt paving and my back was badly scraped.

I ended up with a severe concussion, scalp laceration, broken ribs, heartbeat irregularities, and a colorful collection of scrapes and bruises.

One of the members of my congregation was a neurologist. She stopped by to see me. After looking at the medical chart she said, "It looks like there is no permanent damage. You should recover fully. And it could take six to twelve months." She looked at me as sternly as her kind eyes would allow: "And you'll have to rest a lot during your recovery."

She was generous enough to realize there was no need to comment on the fact that I hadn't been wearing a bike helmet.

Over the next few weeks, about half a dozen members of my congregation gave me brand-new bike helmets along with good-natured and well-deserved scoldings for being so reckless.

The doctor told me there is really no good way to measure the severity of a concussion. But memory loss is an indicator. There were at least eight hours between the moment of reaching for the doorknob and the moment of "coming to" in the hospital room. That is a long time.

The hippocampus cycles through recent experiences as it gradually processes and transfers them to long-term memory in the neocortex. Apparently, my hippocampus was knocked offline. To this day, I have no memory of any of those eight hours. It is as if I hadn't been there at all and went straight from reaching to open the back door to lying in the hospital room.

Because of the severity of the concussion, my memory function came back slowly. I spent much of that summer in a lawn chair in my backyard, reading, sleeping, and healing.

Thankfully, we had a talented intern minister to fill in for me. By fall, I could resume a portion of my ministerial duties.

Six months later a congregant asked me if I was still forgetting things. Think about that question for a moment. How might you answer it?

I said, "I haven't forgotten anything I remember."

In truth I don't think the brain actually heals from such an injury. But the brain is an organic learning machine, which can adapt and compensate for damage.

The Hard Problem

The bike accident and its aftermath raise interesting questions about the nature of awareness and its relationship to the brain, consciousness, and a sense of self. It illustrates how deeply interdependent they can be.

Years ago I was convinced that awareness was a fundamental element in the universe. "Fundamental" means it is its own thing: awareness is not derived from nor made up of anything but awareness.

As a rough analogy, matter and energy were once thought to be fundamentally distinct. Then Albert Einstein proposed they were not with his famous equation $E=mc^2$ (the energy in an object equals the mass of the object multiplied by the speed of light squared). In the years since, his formula has held up to scientific scrutiny.

When it comes to awareness, the comparable question is: "Is awareness fundamentally its own thing or is it the by-product of physical things like brain tissues?"

In the early 1990s the Australian philosopher David Chalmers dubbed this "the Hard Problem." To rephrase it slightly, "How do the physical properties of the brain give rise to the subjective experiences of the mind?" If awareness is not fundamental, the brain is the most promising place to search for the source of awareness in physical material. But it's been darn hard to pin down how that might work.

Part of what makes the Hard Problem hard is there are so many neurological components and mental functions that intertwine. It's difficult to sort them all out. When some key components are missing, the self can seem a little bizarre or disturbing.

For example, after my bicycle accident my wife and son answered my question "What happened?" over and over. But I could not remember what they said or even that they had said anything. They naturally began to worry about who it was that emerged from the mishap. Was I still the same person they had known and loved for many years?

Clearly, I wasn't all there, though I wasn't completely absent either. I was not in a vegetative state. There was somebody home. But was it really the same person? Or did I have a lesser degree of self than they had known? Or a different self?

Rather than look at just the question of memory and a sense of self, I'd like to broaden the focus to include the whole range of components that give rise to the self and consciousness. I don't think the Hard Problem can be adequately addressed without including them all.

Four Propositions

Exploring these elements will suggest four propositions about the self and consciousness. We'll reflect on these four in the coming pages:

They are complex. First, self and consciousness are not simple. They are complex phenomena made up of multiple components that interweave in complex ways. We've looked at many of them in the preceding chapters. We'll go through them in the next few chapters. We can then put them all together. I think this will reveal how complicated they both are. There are degrees and qualities of self just as there are degrees and qualities of consciousness. They are multifaceted phenomena: we have many selves and many consciousnesses.

They wax and wane. Second, the various components of the self and consciousness wax and wane in response to threats that may be either real or imagined, intense or mild. As the components arise and fade, the selves and consciousness also wax and wane, come forth and disappear, focus sharply and fuzz out. Sometimes the effect can be disturbing, as in me asking a simple question over and over.

They have their origins in the body. Third, the self-sense and consciousness arise from the body. Without a human body, human consciousness is not possible. Without a bird body, bird consciousness is not possible. Without a gerbil body, gerbil consciousness is not possible.

This does not rule out the possibility of machine consciousness. We aren't there yet, but if we do get there, machine consciousness will necessarily be different from human, bird, or gerbil consciousness because the underlying physical material would be a machine, not an organic body.

Could such a machine have a sense of self? Perhaps. But it's hard to guess what that might be like.

They are necessarily tied together. Fourth, consciousness and a sense of self seem to be joined at the hip. Without consciousness, there is no self. They co-arise. Once conscious awareness arises, the mind assumes there is something that holds that awareness — i.e. some kind of selfhood.

The Buddha agreed that they are connected but cautioned that the self has no ontological depth — no essence nor substance. It's just a practical and useful metaphor for a shallow phenomenon. He referred to selfhood with images like a bubble, a mirage, or a conjurer's trick. The bubble, mirage, and trick are real, but they have nothing behind them. We have a self but, like a bubble, it's vacuous. Like a mirage or a trick it's not what it appears to be. Self is only a phantom. And if we attach to it, we are likely to suffer because it's empty.

Selfing

At first glance, the self appears to be a unitary thing. Yet under closer examination, it is made up of many components. And those components are actually processes — verbs, not nouns. We *do* selfing more than *are* a self. The self is fluid and arises and fades. The bike accident illustrates how, when just one process breaks down (in this case memory storage) the whole seemingly unified phenomenon of self begins to look weird.

Self and consciousness are all made of nonself components. There is no self-essence buried in all the parts. That is how freedom is found: there is no self to be freed.

Looking Ahead

The remainder of this chapter explores how to work kindly and wisely with the illusion of a unitary self in meditation.

In Chapter 12, we'll break that unity down into the five components described by the Buddha as the five "heaps" or *khandhas*. Each khandha is also a process more than a thing.

The Buddha did not have modern technology and science. So in Chapter 13, we'll look at the self through the eyes of neural science and its much finer delineation of components. We'll look specifically at ten processes.

In Chapter 14, we'll weave them all back together.

The common thread through these chapters is that self is a process, more than a thing. And as Andrew Olendski suggests:

> *Grasping is not something done by the self, but rather self is something done by grasping.*
>
> – Andrew Olendzki[25]

Implications for Meditation

Despite the classical Buddhist description of the self having several khandhas and afflictive emotions, the sense of self often presents as a unitary phenomenon. We experience self as one thing rather than as a bunch of parts. And that sense of self is accompanied by contractions. They can be subtle, but they are there. Often the tightening is accompanied by thinking.

Thinking is an evolutionary adaptation to real or imagined threat— perhaps we left the stove on or it starts to rain while the window is open. It helps to deal with these directly: check the stove; close the window. And if they turn out to be false alarms, we can confidently relax the contraction.

When we relax, the sense of self may loosen up, feel like gossamer, and not so solid or continuous. Until we get used to this fading away, it can be disconcerting. Our system tightens up a little and the old familiar self solidifies. Often, we don't see the relationship between tightening and the

---

[25] Andrew Olendzki, *Unlimiting Mind,* (Wisdom Publications, 2010), p.133.

relatively monolithic self. But this fading and solidifying of self-sense can happen over and over.

But if we do notice the contraction or sense of solidity, we can patiently turn toward it, relax into it, and savor/smile. That helps us see how the sense of self waxes and wanes just like any other phenomenon. In Chapter 5 (p. 59-66) I described these as the Ennobling Practices outlined by the Buddha. To summarize:

1. **Turn toward** the sense of self to understand more clearly what it is and isn't as well as how it operates. Turning toward is not an intellectual analysis. It is just a phenomenon we receive in our direct experience (pp. 59-62).

2. **Relax into** the sense of self to soften any distorting tension. Trying to push tightness away is like trying to put out a fire with gasoline: it makes it worse. So instead, we relax without trying to get rid of anything. Patience and a sense of humor are also helpful (pp. 62-65).

3. **Savor** any good feelings that arise spontaneously. This is our natural wellbeing coming through. If uplifted feelings don't arise on their own, then we **smile** softly. Smiling gently may neurologically trigger happiness, contentment, or other wholesome qualities. It's not wise to force anything. We just raise the corners of the mouth a little and see what happens (pp. 65-66).

As we turn toward, relax into, and savor/smile, the sense of self may lighten up or fade completely.

In other words, we treat the sense of self like any other hindrance to be seen, understood, relaxed, and uplifted. What's important is not whether or not the self or other hindrances arise: this side of enlightenment they will continue to show up. What's important is how we relate to them. We want to see them clearly without identifying with them.

The simplest way to do this is the Three Practices: turn toward, relax into, savor / smile.

If this engenders a growing sense of peace or stillness inside, then we are on a good path. But if we keep getting sidetracked in our practice, an understanding of the khandhas can help get us back on the path.

I explore that in the next chapter.

12

Heaps of Experience: The Buddha's Khandhas

I find it difficult to imagine seeing the world through the eyes of the Buddha, in part because the only language in which I am competent is English. I think and write in English. The language he spoke was Pakrit and the language used to record his teaching was Pāli. English has a higher percentage of nouns than most other languages. Pakrit and Pāli have a higher percentage of verbs than most languages. When his words and thoughts are transcribed into English, many verbs are changed into gerunds or other kinds of nouns.

To me the world is a matrix in which tiny atoms are the building blocks of molecules, which are the building blocks of compounds which are the building blocks of the complex materials that form the stuff of life including you and me, the planets, the stars, and the galaxies. This seems obvious.

But this wasn't obvious to the Buddha. He saw life made up of processes within processes, swirls within swirls, verbs within verbs, motions within motions, energies responding within engeries. He called this "dependent origination" or "dependent co-arising": everything arises and passes dependent upon others arising and passing.

The Buddha did recognize things and nouns, obviously. He said we have a self. But the self is not made of things within things. It is made of processes within processes. In other words, self as a thing is vacuous. He referred to it as a swelling, bubble, or vortex in a moving river. The self is made up of swirls within swirls.

The core of the Buddha's teaching is not a thing but a process — the alleviation of suffering. His diagnosis of suffering is simple and penetrating: clinging leads to personalizing, which leads to suffering.

It's possible to create a sense of self out of just about anything. And we do! We identify with our bodies, personalities, political views, familial roles, occupations, and more. The Buddha used the term khandhas to describe how a sense of self is generated from a few simple distortions in the mind-body system. The khandhas affected by taṇhā map out how this unfolds.

The Pāli word "khandha" means "heaping together," though it is usually translated more genteelly as "aggregate." It is a clumping or collecting of similar experiences. The khandhas form a chain where the first khandha triggers the second, which triggers the third, and so on, up through the fifth khandha. Think of the khandhas as "dependent co-arising lite." Dependent origination has a similar causal chain, with twelves links. The khandhas only have five as shown in Table 3.

Again, the khandhas outline the Buddha's view of selfing as a series of actions within actions. In this chapter we'll go through each of the five khandhas and consider how to use them while meditating on or off the cushion.

Table 3. Khandhas

Khandha	English Translation	Notes
rūpa	living, sensing body; sensations	*phassa* refers to contact between energy and a sensing organ
vedanā	feeling tone	varieties of pleasant, unpleasant, or neutral
saññā	pointers, perception	names, labels
saṅkhāra	concepts, story lines, beliefs	give a sense of solidity and continuity to the self
viññāṇa	awareness, consciousness	disposition, proclivity

1. Sensation

The *rūpa* khandha is the name of the first khandha. In Pāli, "rūpa" means "body." In English, "body" can be alive or dead. But in Pāli, rūpa refers to a living, sensing organism that picks up stimuli from the environment when a sense organ makes contact *(phassa)* with a sense object. So a functional translation of rūpa khandha is "sensing" or "sensation." It's the body-mind *(nāmarūpa)* faculty that is aware and that registers impressions.

When I woke up in the hospital bed after the bicycle accident (pp. 155-160), I didn't know where I was or how I got there. I could see a blurry gray strip across my field of vision, but I didn't know what it was. The first khandha was at work producing visual sensations even though I knew nothing about them. That's rūpa.

In Buddhism there are six senses — five are sensory (seeing, hearing, smelling, tasting, and tactile), and one is mental (thinking, planning, and other nonsensory experiencing). In Buddhism the mind is considered a sensing organ that works with thinking analogous to the way eyes work with seeing.

In meditation, the first khandha is never a problem in and of itself. Sights, sounds, smells, tastes, touch, and thoughts arise naturally and effortlessly from the body. Nature bred us to notice them as part of a survival strategy.

These raw sensations do not include tension (taṇhā). So if tension accompanies them, then we patiently use the Three Practices (turn toward, relax into, savor / smile, pp. 59-66). If these don't work well, then we can use the more detailed Six Rs (Appendix A, pp. 223-229) to get back on track.

2. Feeling Tone

Sensations trigger the second khandha, *vedanā,* or feeling tones, which can be pleasant, unpleasant, or somewhere in between. Vedanā is wired into us biologically, so we have no control over what arises. However, we do have some influence over how we respond, and how we respond affects future vedanā.

There are a wide variety of feeling tones. Vedanā is vulnerable to the distortion of tension (taṇhā). For example, it's easy to believe it is "my feeling" rather than just "a feeling."

Trying to prevent feeling tones from arising is aversion: it makes matters worse. And besides, once a feeling tone has arisen, trying to block it is impossible, because it's already here! Buddhist practice is about seeing what's real, not about trying to bend reality to our wishes. As we saw in Chapter 3, in Buddhism there is no "fake it 'til you make it."

If the feeling tone is pleasant, it is usually easy enough to just relax into it. If it is unpleasant, it may be helpful to turn toward, relax into, and savor / smile.

There are such a wide variety of feeling tones that sometimes we may not be sure which one it is. That's okay. We can use the Three Practices without knowing what the feeling tone is.

If that feels difficult, I've found that vedanā usually falls into one of four broad categories: mad, sad, glad, or scared. If the vedanā falls into one of those general areas, it may be easiest to use the Three Practices.

The khandhas are impersonal and arise simply out of the mind-body system being alive. They are just fine if we relate to them with kindness and wisdom. But that's a big "if" — kindness and wisdom can slip past us as we fall into subtle or not so subtle pulling and pushing, liking and disliking, or more dramatic greed, hatred, and delusion.

3. Perception

Sensations and feeling tones give rise to the third khandha, *saññā*. Saññā is usually translated as "perception," but this can be misleading. In Buddhism, saññā manifests as labels or names that point to an experience: "hot evening," "hospital bed rail," "bicycle," and so on. When I was lying in the hospital bed looking at the blurry strip in my visual field, "bed rail" was not the direct experience itself. It was a label I used to point to the experience.

Words, labels, and pointers are slight abstractions. Knowing they are conceptual helps distinguish what the sense of self is and isn't. Saññā always has at least a little tension.

Voice in the Mind

In meditation, and elsewhere, saññā almost always appears as a voice in the mind. If not a voice, then it may be a spontaneous image.

If this happens often in a particular sitting, we can watch for the voice or image to begin to arise. This allows us to catch it earlier and use the Three Practices. Sometimes we can soften into the voice before the sentence is complete or relax the image before it's clear. With patient practice, we notice the voice before a complete sentence or even a phrase gets out.

With more patience and practice, we may notice a slight thickening or other voices or images in the mind-heart before they have any momentum. We can turn toward, relax into, and savor / smile with that first hint.

We start to realize that the voice is impersonal. With that, the sense of self thins out a little bit more.

If the voice or images slip past us, our mind may go into the fourth khandha.

4. Constructs

Sañña triggers *saṅkhāra,* the fourth khandha, which are even more abstract and complex. Saṅkhāra are concepts, story lines, beliefs, and ideas. The term literally means an action that is formed or shaped by the mind. They are larger mental constructs than the simple pointers of the saññā khandha. Ideas, beliefs, and stories are real, but they aren't tangible. With saṅkhāra we have moved completely away from the sensory realm, where we started and into the mental realm.

My story about the bicycle accident is itself a multilayered construct meant to point to something real. The story about the trolls using me for a soccer ball is also saṅkhāra, but in this case it was intended to convey what I was feeling (vedanā) rather than actual events.

In meditation, sometimes ideas and ruminations just roll along. If so, it's important to not get caught up in aversion or clinging to them. It can help to shift attention from the content of the stories and beliefs to the processes in the mind (thinking, daydreaming, planning, etc.) or the feeling tone of the field of awareness that is observing.

We all have slightly different ways of responding to stress and habitual ways in which saṅkhāra appear. As we become more familiar with our systems, we are into the territory of the fifth khandha.

Meanwhile, saṅkhāra may itself generate a feeling tone (vedanā) of solidity and continuity, which can contribute to the sense of self and make it feel solid and continuous.

5. Disposition

The fifth or *viññāṇa* khandha is a little different from the others. It is more complex and nuanced. And it does not come straight out of the previous khandha.

Viññāṇa is usually translated as "consciousness." But consciousness has several meanings. One is "awareness," as in "he lost consciousness," which is synonymous with "he lost awareness." Another meaning is a point of view, way of thinking, or disposition as in "eco-consciousness," "feminist consciousness," "conservative consciousness," or "progressive consciousness." In Buddhism, viññāṇa has both meanings.

Viññāṇa as awareness is part of all the other khandhas. Without it we would not know what we see, hear, smell, taste, touch, or think. We would not know the feeling tones, perceptions, concepts, stories, and so on.

But viññāṇa is not neutral. It has opinions. It colors the way we perceive. It's affected by our disposition. It has a point of view and assigns value to experience.

I became starkly aware of how distorted one's experience can be when I was an undergraduate at the University of Wisconsin at the height of the Vietnam War. I played an active role on a student-strike committee during the protests. For the first time in my life, I had a front-row seat at events that were reaching the attention of the national media.

The reports on television and in newspapers were very different from what I knew was happening on the ground. The reports seemed to reflect the personality of the reporters more than they did actual events. I didn't believe this was deliberate deception. Journalists couldn't help but be predisposed to seeing things from their own perspectives.

It was unsettling to realize that most of my understandings of the larger world came through the same media. Did my views and opinions have more to do with the consciousness of reporters than with the actual world events?

Today I understand better the neurology behind this. As short-term memory in the hippocampus is transcribed into long-term memory in the neocortex, where it is consolidated and processed. If we don't think events are very important, a lot of the details are compressed or eliminated — it doesn't make biological sense to use up precious long-term storage with things that aren't important.

Additionally, the memories stored in the cortex include more than just raw events. They include the vedanā, saññā, saṅkhāra, and viññāṇa (feeling tones, pointers, concepts, and dispositions) that arose with the sensations. Our feelings, disposition, thoughts, and all the rest shape our memory in ways we cannot prevent: it's biological. Knowing our own disposition doesn't stop the combining, shaping, and editing. There is simply no way we can have purely objective views even if we want them. But taking a humbler view of our memories and beliefs can move us in the direction of greater clarity. We'll take a closer look at this in Chapter 13 (pp. 193-195) when we look deeper into the role of memory in consciousness and the sense of self.

In meditation, viññāṇa can manifest as awareness or as disposition. Awareness is part of the other khandhas. But disposition is something that repeats often. Since we have different dispositions, it will not be the same for each of us.

For example, fretfulness and explaining are two patterns that show up often in my practice (p. 25). Fretfulness is covered by the second khandha, vedanā. And explanations are covered by the fourth khandha, saṅkhāra. I understand their origins in my psychological history. But beyond a certain point, the fretfulness and explaining become mental habits with their own momentum. In other words, they become something I'm prone to — part of my disposition.

Knowing my own disposition makes it easier for me to be sensitive to fretfulness or explaining as they arise: hence I can use the Three Practices sooner.

As I do this, the stories and explanations break up into shorter phrases or quicker flashes of images. They no longer fit into a larger story and have very little charge. Some of the sense of solidity and continuity recedes.

I may be tempted to fit the quick words, quiet voices, and subtle flashes of images into a larger pattern. Over the years

I've learned how *unhelpful* this is. It reinforces the third and fourth khandhas by creating more pointers, stories, and ideas.

So I let the words, voices, and images flash through without resistance and without making a big deal about them. They gradually fade into deeper silence on their own.

Summary

The Buddha used the khandhas to describe the ways distortion can create a sense of self. He rarely described exactly what the khandhas were. Perhaps he trusted that his listeners were familiar with them already. He merely described the distortions that warp the khandhas.

Each khandha can create specific kinds of distortion to look for in meditation or in normal life. These arise in the second through the fifth khandha. The first khandha — raw sensation — has relatively little distortion. However, vedanā (feeling tone), when accompanied by the tension of clinging or aversion, can be warped to some degree. That distortion can infect saññā (words and pointers) with a sense of solidity or continuity. This can lead to false concepts and beliefs (saṅkhāra) such as "This is me; this is mine; this is myself." And these concepts can infect our disposition (viññāṇa) with a tendency to color all we see with a sense of self or identity.

Together these create an operational sense of self with small or large distortions.

So working with the khandhas in meditation can be as simple as watching for tension, voices or images in the mind, sense of solidity or continuity, ideas about self or identity, and disposition. If we see any of these, we turn toward, relax into, and savor/smile.

However, when I look inside myself in meditation or otherwise, I often see a more complex range of phenomena than the monolithic self or the generalized distortions of the khandhas. From a neurological perspective, there are other factors that get entangled. None of these negate the Buddha's analysis or the effectiveness of his Three Ennobling Practices.

But paradoxically, we tend to identify with things we don't see clearly. If there is anger in my system and I see it very clearly, I'm apt to say, "I *have* anger." But if I don't see it so clearly, I'm more likely to say "I *am* angry." We personalize it and make it part of ourselves. The Buddha's khandhas can help us to see clearly and objectively. However, khandhas are a little foreign to us, living, as we do, twenty-six hundred years later. And they lack some of the specific signs, which may be a little different for each of us. It may be helpful to examine our own experience and see what particular signs make up our sense of self.

We'll untangle some of these particulars in the next chapter and see how the Ennobling Practices can be used with them.

13

Untangling the Self: From Monolith to Motley Crew

Tangled within, tangled without,
Creatures are tangled in tangles.
And so I ask you, Gautama —
Who can untangle this tangle?

— the Buddha
Samyutta Nikāya 1.23[26]

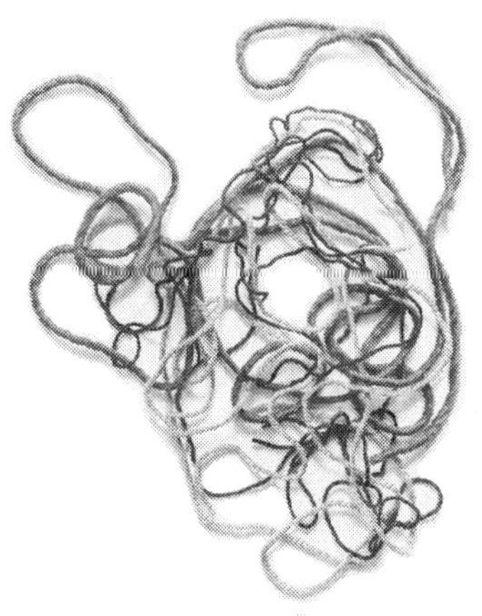

The self often appears to be monolithic and self-contained. However, when we look deeper, we begin to see a motley crew rambling around. Or, to use a different metaphor, we see different strands of thread tangled together. In the last chapter we used the Buddha's five khandhas to help untangle some of those tangles.

There have been many of medical advances since Gautama the Buddha wandered along the Ganges River twenty-six hundred years ago: X-ray, fMRIs, neural surgery,

[26] Adapted from translation by Bhikkhu Sujato.

pharmacology, and more. Modern science gives fresh hints about the nature of self and consciousness. While they don't clash with the Buddha's insights, in some areas they bring details and specificity that goes beyond what was known in his time. Let's continue to untangle the tangles by returning to the neural science.

As we saw with the khandhas, "self" is not a single phenomenon but a constellation of processes. These threads are intertwined. The same is true of the neurological processes. Yet it may help to get to know them separately before looking at how they interweave in the next chapter.

We've reflected on many of these threads in earlier chapters. In those cases, I'll just review their most salient features as we consider these ten strands:

Homeostatic balance
Homeostatic imbalance
Felt sense
Complexity
Actions to restore homeostasis
Free will
Internal maps
Protagonist
Memory
Nondual presence

These are not entirely distinct from one another: some overlap. Some may be experienced directly while others can be inferred from experience and may seem abstract. Meditation begins with direct experience rather than abstractions. So as we go through these, we'll unpack them enough to reveal the felt experience(s) from which they emerge.

Homeostasis and a Mug of Tea

The sense of self and consciousness have humble beginnings: they start with nonverbal sensing that is simple, grounded in the body, and the by-product of homeostasis. For example:

I was sitting on the patio one morning with a mug of tea. Birds sang in the background. The air was cool on my skin and the sun felt warm. There was very little going on inside: my mind was quiet and my sense of self floated lightly in the background.

Then my homeostatic fluid balance went a little off: I felt thirsty. Sipping the tea brought the balance back. Then I put the mug down and gently slid back to sitting in the morning sunlight and enjoying the cool air.

A few minutes later, my cat, Lila, walked onto the patio, sat down a few feet away, and quietly mewed. My attention perked up: "What does she want?" She has Maine coon genes that make her very social. So I patted my lap to signal she was welcome. She jumped up, turned around twice, snuggled down, and purred softly as I stroked her a few times.

I relaxed back into the morning ambiance. Self and consciousness became faint. When there is very little going on inside, I call that "peacefulness" or "wellbeing." Or I don't even think about it — I simply enjoy.

Then my consciousness thickened a little. A quiet urgency came up inside: "I've got a lot to do today including all those emails. I should probably get going." My sense of self became denser and pulled my attention.

I also felt pulled to stay with the peaceful morning. I lingered a few minutes to finish my tea before moving inside to check my calendar and emails.

Notice how the sense of self waxed and waned. Usually we notice a sense of self only when it is dense. It needs a stable point of reference: a sense of constancy rooted in the body.

However, like everyone else, my body has changed a great deal over the years: height, weight, hairline, musculature, injury and healing, sickness and health, and more. But I still have a sense that there is a unitary self that has gone through all those changes. That unity comes from the parts of the body that change the least: homeostatic variables that must stay within a narrow range if we are to stay alive and healthy. Those are found mostly in our viscera: blood pressure, body temperature, tissue hydration, blood sugar levels, heart rate, respiration, and so forth. By keeping those relatively steady, they provide a sense of stability beneath all the fluctuations and changes.

The contrast between that stability and everything else morphing, shifting, and evolving gives us the feeling of a solid self deep inside. When I look at old pictures of me, I think, "Yep. The same old Doug was in there." Our sense of self is not rooted in the world around us, or in all the things that change in our bodies. It is rooted deep in the inner homeostatic constancies that are maintained as long as we are alive.

Homeostatic balance may not be obvious in meditation or daily life. However, if we've been out of balance and are returning to a viable range, we often feel good. We enjoy a glass of cool water, the bite of an apple, the smile of a friend, the pleasure of a moment of clarity. These good feelings don't need to be either held on to or pushed away. We simply relax into them.

However, when homeostatic variables have remained in a viable range for a while, we are often unaware of them. The funny thing about homeostasis is that we may not feel it if it is balanced and there's nothing to be done. There may be a diffuse sense of wellbeing or generalized contentment — like on the patio with a mug of tea and my cat. That is our natural resting place. We tend to naturally savor those moments. And that's just fine.

However, homeostatic imbalances are a different story.

Homeostatic Imbalances

Simple organisms have simple balances maintained by simple reflexes. Poke an amoeba and it pulls away. I doubt it thinks about it — without a nervous system it is incapable of contemplating its circumstances. It simply reacts out of blind instinct. It has no sense of self and no consciousness.

But the situation is different with complex organisms. As I noted, they have many homeostatic variables and reflexes. Sometimes one homeostatic need conflicts with another. On that afternoon walk on the shore with my friend (pp. 103-105), various homeostatic needs pulled me in different directions: for food, warmth, rest, exercise, companionship, care, and more.

A gentler version of those dynamics arose with my morning tea on the patio with Lila. The sense of being thirsty intruded a bit on the peacefulness. I can't even tell you exactly what that thirst felt like, only that I knew I needed fluid. And that was enough to nudge me to drink.

Meanwhile, I doubt that Lila thought, "I'm lonely and I'll tell my human to do something about it." But she felt it diffusely enough to quietly meow. And it triggered in me the affective emotion of CARE (Chapter 2, pp. 22-23). It nudged me to tend to Lila. (I do like living in a multispecies family.) It's also hard for me to describe precisely the pull that drew me to leave the porch and go inside, though it is easy to say what I did about it. The content was symbolized by calendar crunch and email pileup. The homeostatic imbalance felt like a blend of urgency and worry.

While homeostasis gives an anchor to the sense of a continuous self, homeostatic imbalances have the opposite effect — they leave us feeling that we are not ourselves or not the self we want to be. Something seems wrong.

In meditation, imbalances are felt as discomfort. It might be a mild annoyance, searing pain, or something in between. It might be physical, emotional, or mental discomfort, or some mix of them. But it always has a negative valence: we feel hungry, thirsty, lonely, feverish, confused, etc. There are lots of ways to feel bad. They grab our attention and motivate us to do something.

If the imbalance is about something that reasonably needs attention now (e.g., I have to use the bathroom, or I forgot a friend was coming over and now the doorbell is ringing), then it may be wise to get up and act. However, if there is nothing reasonable to be done or if the action can wait for later, then we use the Three Practices (turning toward, relaxing into, and savoring/smiling) and continue our meditation.

Felt Sense

In academic philosophy, the pulls, draws, and nudges of homeostatic imbalances might be called "negative qualia." The word "qualia" refers to the subjective aspects of experience. In contrast, objective aspects are publicly observable. On the walk on the beach and on the patio, objective elements included my friend, the ocean, the sunlight, the vendor stalls, the blue sky, the mug of tea, Lila, and more. These were observable by anyone in the vicinity. However, hunger, thirst, the feeling of being housebound, and anxiousness I felt to check my emails could only be known internally. They were subjective qualia.

A less academic term for qualia is "felt sense." Felt sense is the subjective quality we can feel and sense but may not be able to verbalize adequately. They may be hard to put into words. Imagine trying to describe the difference between hunger and thirst to someone who has experienced neither. We could say, "They are the feelings that arise when we have had no food or water for a long time." But that *merely points* to the experience without saying *what it is*.

The old adage declares, "It takes a finger to point to the moon, but woe to the person who mistakes the finger for the moon." Sometimes we can point to qualia. But if the person has never experienced hunger or thirst, they won't know what we are pointing to.

Qualia, or felt sense, shows up a lot in our lives, including in meditation. It's something that we complex organisms feel. It's not the content of awareness but the texture, mood, or quality of it. Sometimes awareness may be indistinct and fuzzy. It may be no more than the thought "I'm thirsty" or "I'm hungry." It only has to be strong enough to get us to do something. Then it has done its job.

The pull is uncomfortable. It may be intense or mild, physical, emotional, or mental. This pull is also where we become conscious — it is no longer a paramecium reflex but a conscious sense of self that gives us a reference for reflecting on our situation and what to do about it — e.g., "I'm hungry."

Even though hunger, thirst, loneliness, etc., all have negative valences, they have very different qualia. The best we can do is say what they are like. But we cannot say exactly what they are. Yet the experiences are so simple as to seem obvious.

In meditation we may never see something we would describe as a "homeostatic imbalance." But we will feel discomfort to varying degrees. These are the signs of being out of balance. If they capture our attention, we can remind ourselves that they are impersonal as we engage the Three Practices.

Felt sense cannot be felt from a distance. It's up close and personal. We can't deal with it fully if it is only an intellectual construct. To know it, we have to merge with it rather than standing aloof.

You may remember Ava (pp. 89-92), who never experienced pain or upset. It was likely that she would simply waste away blissfully before ever having had a chance to pass on her genes.

By themselves, homeostatic balances and felt sense are not enough to create a full sense of self. But without them, there is nothing stable that can ground our awareness or sense of self.

Complexity

Another component of self and consciousness is complexity. As described in Chapter 8 (pp. 101-105), complex organisms often have many homeostatic balances competing for a resolution at once. This complexity is key to what gives rise to consciousness as well as to a sense of self. If the perception of complexity is diminished because of disease or damage to specific parts of the brain, the sense of self and consciousness diminish as well.

When complexity arises in meditation, it helps to let the attention rest on the felt sense itself rather than trying to analyze it. Analysis puts us in objective mode and out of reach of subjective felt sense. And if the felt sense is indistinct, it is best to just notice how it feels rather than trying to make it more distinct. We may have a felt sense that is very knowable though hard to put into words.

Complexity can also show up as the mind jumping from topic to topic, image to image, from one snippet of a conversation to another. Or there may be many things going on at once.

Rather than trying to quiet or soothe the mind-heart, we can relax into the flow, even if it's jumpy. From this acceptance we can look for the stillness behind the movements in the mind. If we notice a stillness, we let everything be as it is and relax into the quiet that was already there.

A welcoming attitude toward whatever arises does little to change this moment but has a calming effect on the following moments. So it helps to *welcome rather than entangle, to observe rather than control,* and *to let the mind quiet itself in its own time.*

Actions to Restore Homeostasis

When we feel the pull or a push of a homeostatic imbalance, we often act. The felt sense may be very subtle. But actions are apparent. We can sense them with more clarity. They strengthen both the sense of self and consciousness.

The action that restores a homeostatic imbalance has its own felt sense as well. It may have a quality and texture that is different from the sense of imbalance. Again, it can be known in our experience, though it may be difficult to put into words that adequately describe it to someone who has never done those actions.

Free Will

Consciousness creates a pause between several competing homeostatic needs and the urges to bring them into balance (pp. 101-105). Out of this comes free will — the ability to choose an action.

Action gives rise to a sense of agency — we can be the instrument of some action. Complex organisms have a choice to act or not. That is the whole point! There may be conflicting actions: Do I walk on the beach or seek shelter? Do I enjoy my tea and cat a little longer or check the emails? Free will and agency strengthen the sense of self and bring conscious awareness to the surface.

People who are enslaved, imprisoned, or dominated by another, may feel less than whole. When free will is diminished, our sense of self is diminished. The slave who runs away, the prisoner who escapes, the dominated person who rebels has their sense of self strengthened by acting against an outside force.

Reflexes and Free Will

It may be difficult to tell from the outside if a creature's action is based on free will or just blind reflex. Some simple creatures can act quite intelligently without a mind — hence no sense of self and no consciousness.

Consider the nematode. Biologically, these worms have been quite successful: over a million different species spread through every habit on the planet. Like any living creature, a nematode called *Caenorhabditis elegans* (or *C. elegans*) needs to eat in order to survive. It may feed alone or in groups. However, if food is scarce, if other creatures are around, or if there are signs of danger, it will only feed in a group. It appears to have social awareness, intentional cooperation, altruistic motives, and the capacity to figure out that there is safety in numbers.

But *C. elegans* has no brain and only about three hundred neurons in a chain of ganglia. It's only a worm! It has no mind, no consciousness, no sense of self, and therefore no free will. Its actions are intelligent but initiated by reflexes that evolved from evolutionary laws.

Some of the implications of nematodes are humbling. Our 86 billion-neuron brains may deserve less credit than we think. Many aspects of our intelligence do not come out of our vast neocortex but out of evolutionary inheritance from simple, mindless, ancient ancestors.

Our large cortex is indeed beautiful and affords us a vast amount of flexibility, cognitive processing, and free will that simpler creatures lack. But some of our intelligence has ancient roots. We have more in common with nematodes and other simple creatures than we might imagine. The interdependent web of life is indeed interdependent.

Free Will and Determinism

Note that the Buddha believed neither in absolute free will (that we are unconstrained in the choices we make) nor in absolute determinism (that our path is already set). Rather, as in so many other areas, he believed in a middle way between these two extremes, where we are free to choose, but where our choices are encumbered by our past actions and present circumstances, including genetics, culture, race, gender, and much more. Paradoxically, the more we are aware of the hidden influences in our lives, the freer we are to go against those influences if we so choose. But, this side of enlightenment, the forces of dependent origination (*paṭiccasamuppāda)* influence our lives.

Internal Maps

We already noted how felt sense gives us the ability to reflect on our situation, figure out alternatives, and make choices as to how to act. To do this, we need the ability to represent our situation internally.

As we saw in Chapters 8 and 9, the brain is a mapmaking machine. We make cognitive maps of the world around us and respond to those internal representations more than to what's "out there." The brain is locked away in the skull (pp. 119-122). It can respond faster because these "maps" are always available, whereas the external world is a scramble of impressions and it takes time to make sense of them on the fly.

A simple example of this is my editing of the draft of this book. I am very poor at catching my own typos because I am so familiar with what I want to say that as I read, I inadvertently pay more attention to what's in my mind than to what's on the page. It takes less effort to "read" from my brain than from the computer screen in front of me. There can be whole words missing on the page and I skip right over them because I can "see" them in my mind.

Another example of paying more attention to internal maps was expecting my friend to arrive in a blue car and being a little startled when someone else (the "wrong person") stepped out of the car (p. 129).

Protagonist

One object on the map is "me." Yet I am different from any other object: I am the protagonist in the center of my experience.

If I see a hawk gliding lazily above without it seeing me, my observation does not affect the hawk. But if I observe myself, I can't avoid seeing me! The perception arises inside my body: I am inside my perception of me. I am both the object known and the knower. This creates a neural loop whereby I become the protagonist at the center of my experience including me as my protagonist.

But it's a fiction produced by the brain's mapping capacities. The brain has no single structure that serves as an executive director. The decisions the brain makes use distributive intelligence rather than an organic command and control center.

Nevertheless, we have a subjective experience of a self as a solid entity in charge — at least until we look closely and it all comes apart.

I suspect that the sense of self evolved from natural selection: creatures who believed they were a protagonist to be protected were more likely to survive a dangerous situation than creatures who had a more casual relationship to their organism.

My cat, Lila, also has a sense of self. But with neither words nor a large cerebral cortex, her protagonist is simpler and more instinct driven. Yet she still has a significant sense of self.

Efferent Copy

The sense of a protagonist is reinforced by other elements of our neural wiring. For example, consider the so-called efferent-copy neurons.

We have both afferent and efferent neurons. Afferent neurons carry information from sensory receptors toward the central nervous system. Efferent neurons carry motor signals away from the central nervous system to other body parts to initiate actions.

As the efferent neurons leave the brain, they split. One side of the split goes to various muscles or glands in the body. The other side of the split — the so-called efferent-copy — loops back into the brain. For example, if I move my arm, the efferent signal goes to the relevant arm muscles while the efferent copy goes back to the part of the brain that senses movement in that arm muscle.

The efferent copy gives the brain a split-second warning that it is about to feel the arm muscle move. This warning dampens the incoming sensory information. I don't feel it as strongly as I would if I were completely relaxed and you moved my arm for me.

Thus, sensory signals about movements that are generated internally are felt differently than the same signals generated externally. This is very helpful. If I intentionally move my arm, I probably don't want to do anything about those sensations. But if you move my arm against my will, that is a very different situation. I might want to do something about it.

The poster child for the effect of the efferent copy is the tickle reflex. If I am ticklish and you rub my sides in a certain way, I laugh. I don't choose to do so. But I can't help it, because it's a reflex. But if I rub my own sides in the same way, I don't laugh. I cannot tickle myself because the efferent copy dampens the tickle reflex when I try to self-administer it.

The efferent copy is an example of how the body's neurological response to our protagonist ("me") is different from how we response to a non-protagonist ("you").

In Chapter 11 we explored some meditation practices that work with the overall sense of self (pp. 164-166). These practices can also be used with the protagonist. The internal sense of self can be treated as a protagonist who might not be who we really are.

Memory

The capacity to create maps and a protagonist requires memory. The mind is a flow of representations of the world around us and our responses to it — a "flow of consciousness." Memory is a huge component of mind, consciousness, and self-sense.

But memory is so ubiquitous that it's easy to take it for granted — it's easy to underestimate how complex, fragile, and changeable it is.

We live four blocks from an elementary school. Every school day children walk by our home. But I can't remember if I actually saw kids yesterday. However I do remember quite well moving into the dorms at the University of Wisconsin over fifty years ago.

Memory is not passive. Things we don't value fade more quickly than things we care about.

Short-term memories circulate through the hippocampus for days and can remain there as long as a month. But gradually memory traces are transferred to the neocortex. As they are transcribed, they are edited, consolidated, and modified. Police know that eyewitnesses can be unreliable because emotional charge can inflate, deflate, and edit memories or conflate imagination with recall. Our memories are not passive representations.

Furthermore, if events are similar, rather than store a copy of each instance, the brain says in effect, "That's a lot of work. Those memories are similar. It's more efficient to save one copy and reference it multiple times."

I have two eggs and a protein shake for breakfast on most mornings. But I'm not sure how I cooked the eggs or what fruit I used in the shakes each morning this week. They all blend together, so to speak.

Nevertheless, memory is a vital part of who we sense ourselves to be. When my bike accident took my hippocampus offline (pp. 157-160), I couldn't form memories for many hours. The momentum of old memories continued, but I was unable to update them. I am told I seemed more like a simple child — a curious kid, happy to be present — so it wasn't all bad for me. But it was hard for those around me to figure out who I was and how to adjust to this new person. Relational homeostatic variables were out of their normal range. It was disconcerting.

To be sure, though I couldn't form new memories, I hadn't lost the old ones. I remembered events from first thing that morning and back many years. I could speak, which requires remembering words and syntax. I knew my family. I just couldn't retain new memories for more than a few minutes.

Diseases like dementia can erase old memories. When the damage is deep enough, people forget who they are and may have large shifts in personality — their sense of self is changed, sometimes dramatically. In severe cases, they lose speech and any sense of who or where they are.

Nondual Presence

As I understand it, the goal of Buddhist meditation is to be present with what is most real in each moment. As simple as that sounds, it's not easy because the present can subtly be quite complex.

For example, we often conflate consciousness with wakefulness. But we can be unawake and conscious in the same moment. And we do so every day. We call it "dreaming."

We can also be awake and unconsciousness at the same moment. This is rarer. But most of us have had the experience of waking up from a deep sleep and, for a moment, not remembering where we are, what day it is, what time of day it is, or maybe even who we are. Usually this only lasts for a few seconds until consciousness spontaneously comes online and our sense of self reenters the picture along with our story and time-and-place orientation. But for a few seconds we had been awake and unconscious.

A much rarer condition is called a vegetative state, in which a person is completely unresponsive for days or months. Yet, when their brain arousal is measured by an EEG or direct brain stimulation, we see that the person continues to go through periods of brain activity identical to waking and sleeping cycles. I shudder to think of what that must be like internally.

But probably the most common of these brain states is "nondual awareness" or simply "indiscriminate awareness."

We visited nondual awareness in Chapters 6 and 8 (pp. 74, 115).

For example, I might admire someone and be mad at them at the same time. For the sake of logical consistency, I might push one feeling out of my mind — I become conscious of admiration and unconscious of anger. Or vice versa. Of course, unconscious feelings still affect me. They hide behind a bush and leap out when my guard is down: They can betray their presence through my choice of words or vocal tones.

We experience logical inconsistency all the time. I may feel dispassionate about my situation and at the same time wish it was different. I may support my child's forthrightness and at the same time want to protect him from the blowback I see coming.

With our 86 billon neurons, we are perfectly capable of having many inner thoughts and feelings at the same time, even if some conflict with others.

Nondual awareness allows for contradictory thoughts and feelings. And disconcerting though it may be, it leaves room for the disquiet as well. We are simply present with what is most real in this moment.

Nondual awareness could also be called "indiscriminate awareness" because it doesn't favor one thing over another. Becoming accustomed to nondual/indiscriminate awareness, can be a relief. We aren't wasting energy trying to control things we cannot control.

This does not mean we have to act one way or another. We still have choices over what we say or do. There may be some wisdom in both choices. That's for wisdom to sort out.

The important point is that things can go on in the mind without us being conscious of them: we can know things without knowing what we know. And this process can be dynamic.

For example, I often do my best writing in my sleep. If I'm stuck on a problem in a manuscript, I may drop the whole thing and go to bed. In the morning when I wake up, sometimes a solution is in my head. It's as if my brain kept working on it while my conscious awareness was turned off.

Both meditation and psychotherapy value waking up certain kinds of unconscious knowing. We refer to this as "insight." When insights emerge, they often feel familiar — more like remembering than discovering something new. They feel like waking up.

In meditation, we can cultivate nondual/indiscriminate awareness by being receptive. Rather than trying to concentrate attention or scrutinizing our experience, we sit back and let awareness come to us. We openly receive whatever shows up. If our perception is fuzzy, rather than trying to sharpen it, we let the fuzziness be as it is and just notice it.

Deeper insights often arise from this receptivity more than from intentional poking around. Part of the problem with focused investigation is that when we are looking for something, we have an expectation. That expectation can cloud our ability to see that which is novel.

To repeat Suzuki Roshi (p. 150):

If your mind is empty, it is ready for anything;
it is open to everything.
In the beginner's mind there are many possibilities;
in the expert's mind there are few.

Not Personal

In this chapter we've looked at ten of the salient features or processes that come together to create a sense of self from the perspective of neuroscience. These are: *homeostatic balance, homeostatic imbalance, felt sense, complexity, actions to restore homeostasis, free will, internal maps, protagonist, memory,* and *nondual presence.*

We could sort these ten components into even finer distinctions or find whole new ones. But hopefully ten is enough to make the points that the enlightened mind is

- Not monolithic
- Composed of nonself elements
- Not attached to a protagonist or any other self
- Comfortable with contradiction
- Cannot imagine taking things personally

14

Shadows in a Mirror: Constructing Selves

In Chapter 12 we examined how the Buddha broke down the sense of self into five nonself "heaps," or "aggregates." In Chapter 13 we saw how neural science untangled ten threads that contribute to consciousness and a sense of self. In this chapter we'll deepen these reflections by looking at how they can be woven back together into developmental stages that could be called:

- **Protoself** — the building blocks of selfhood
- **Core self** — the emerging sense of "me"
- **Autobiographical self** — the storyline of self
- **Multiple selves** — the many personalities we all have
- **Nonself** — self emerges from and fades into emptiness

The names for the first three come from the work of Antonio Damasio.[27] The fourth is from Eugene Gendlin.[28] And the last is from the Buddha's teachings.

---

[27] Antonio Damasio, *Self Comes to Mind: Constructing the Conscious Brain* (Vintage Books, 2010).

[28] Eugene T. Gendlin, *Focusing* (Bantam Books, 1978, 1981).

These stages map loosely but not precisely onto the Buddha's khandha as illustrated in Table 4.

Table 4. Developmental Stages of Self

Stages of Self	Khandhas of the Buddha
Protoself	1. Rūpa: sensation
Core self	2. Vedanā: feeling tone
Autobiographical self	3. Saññā: perception 4. Saṅkhāra: constructs
Multiple selves	5. Viññāṇa: dispositions
Nonself	Anattā: nonself

Notice that two of the khandhas — saññā and saṅkhāra — are both part the autobiographical self. Also notice that anattā or nonself is beyond the khandhas even though it's an important part of the Buddha's teachings. As we explore further, I think it will become clear that the differences between the stages of self and the khandhas are conceptual rather than substantive.

Since we've looked at most of the elements of the first two developmental stages in the last chapter, we'll do a quick review of how they come together. Then we'll take a longer look at the later stages with a special emphasis on the last: anattā or nonself. The Buddha contended that even though the phenomenon of self is real and socially useful, any sense of an enduring, independent self behind these stages is a figment of our imaginations. Ultimately, self and all its components are just shadows in a mirror: we can perceive them, but they are not substantial. In the end, the light of wise awareness dispels them all.

Protoself

Homeostatic Balance + Homeostatic Imbalance + Felt Sense + Complexity + Actions to Restore Homeostasis

The first stage is the protoself. It corresponds roughly to the rūpa khandha or raw sensations.

It is a precursor to a sense of self and consists of essential building blocks of a full self-sense. These include the first five components described in Chapter 13: homeostatic balance, homeostatic imbalance, felt sense, complexity, and actions to restore homeostasis.

As we've seen (p. 101-107), complex creatures have so many homeostatic variables that several may go out of balance at the same time. The organism must decide which to deal with first. In simpler creatures, imbalances are handled by unconscious reflexes. In complex creatures, these imbalances generate discomfort or pain in various forms. The important point is that these are felt as conscious experiences that motivate differing actions.

Core Self

Proto Self + Free Will + Internal Maps + Protagonist

The second stage is the core self. It is roughly similar to vedanā or the second khandha of feeling tone.

The protoself does not disappear as the more sophisticated stage emerges. Rather, the core self draws on the protoself and adds to it free will, internal maps, and a protagonist.

Because the brain resides in isolation inside the skull, we do not experience the world directly (p. 119-122). The brain receives highly coded neural signals through its Markov blankets (p. 122). We saw how the brain uses these signals to construct an internal map of the world. During construction of those maps, the incoming signals are consolidated, edited, filtered, slanted by disposition, and so forth. The inner maps never match the external world precisely. They only have to be good enough for the organism to get around.

The protagonist is one of the objects on the internal map. But it is different from the other objects in that the act of perception affects the perceiver while the disposition of the perceiver affects the perception. This creates a unique feedback loop. The efferent copy (pp. 192-193) and other mechanisms add to this.

Autobiographical Self

Core Self + Memory

The third stage is the autobiographical self. It roughly includes both the third and fourth khandha: saññā or perceptions and saṅkhāra or constructs. Saññā is more than raw sensation. It includes a simple conceptual label used to name the experience. Saṅkhāra, as we saw earlier, are more elaborate constructs we use to create a map of the world and ourself in that map.

The autobiographical self draws on both the protoself and the core self. To these it adds memory: now the protagonist has a story line. Memory provides a past to ruminate on and a future to anticipate. From lessons learned, it develops values and expectations of what's coming. This is a fully developed sense of self.

The autobiographical self is not always active. It can sit on the sidelines and let the core self have full sway. My time sitting on the patio with a mug of tea is an example of the autobiographical self sitting in the background, even during my encounters with thirst and my cat. However, as I started to worry about emails and a crowded calendar, the autobiographical self arose out of its slumber and settled into the driver's seat.

Multiple Selves

Autobiographical Self + Autobiographical Self + …

The autobiographical self can be a platform from which other selves arise with different personalities and inclinations. In the khandhas, these are called *viññāṇa*. Viññāṇa can be translated as "constructs." But in this case, they are not just any constructs but the ones we carry around. They help shape how we see and respond to the world. This function is better captured by the English word "disposition." Viññāṇa could also be called "personality" or "character structure.

Antonio Damasio[29] talks about a *spiritual self* with refined sensing, a *social self* that focuses more on relationships, and so on. Each of us has a collection of selves specific to us.

One of the differences between the Buddha's teaching and some modern schools of psychology is that the Buddha talks about *a self* while some psychologies talk about *several selves* in the same person.

For example, the self that I experience when I'm playing with my grandchildren is very different from the self that talks with clients or meditators. That self is different from the self who delivers Dhammā talks, who is different from the self walking in the woods near my home, who is different from the self spending a quiet evening with my wife, who is different from the self in a march for social justice, who is different from the self grocery shopping. Most of us have somewhere between ten and twenty selves. Gendlin calls them "personas."[30] They

---

[29] Antonio Damasio, *Self Comes to Mind* (Vintage Books, 2010).

[30] Eugene T. Gendlin, *Focusing* (Bantam Books, 1978, 1981).

are personalities with different sets of manners, desires, fears, agendas, and attitudes. Depending on the situation at any given moment, we may shift fluidly in and out of these to adjust to our circumstances.

Eugene Gendlin developed a style of psychotherapy based on getting to know these various personas.[31] These selves should not be confused with multiple personality disorder, which usually arises out of abuse or severe mistreatment. Rather they are quite normal in healthy, stable people.

Since the selves have different needs and tendencies, it can be helpful to become familiar with all of them so that we can know what they care about and we can take them into account. Deep contentment is probably not possible when one or more of them is neglected.

Exploring these different personas can be rich and rewarding, but it's beyond the scope of this book. However, for our purposes here, it's important to note that we do have many viññāṇa, not just one. Each arises and passes depending on our circumstances. We begin to notice that in the larger interdependent web of life, none of them last. They all dependently arise and eventually fade. None are permanent. As this becomes more obvious, we begin to realize that ultimately there is no lasting self whatsoever.

Nonself

This brings us to the Buddha's core teachings on anattā or nonself. It may be one of the most confusing and misunderstood elements of his teachings. Part of the difficulty is that he was not trying to lay out religious doctrines or

---

[31] While Eugene Gendlin was primarily a researcher rather than a meditator or clinical psychologist, his work has implications for the experience of selfhood in both meditative and clinical contexts.

philosophical constructs. Rather, he was describing a phenomenology of direct experience. He believed that by carefully examining our actual experiences, we could learn enough to free ourselves from suffering.

To get a feel for this, imagine a rainstorm. When clouds, moisture, temperature, and wind are in the right proportions, a storm ensues. When the conditions are not right, there is no storm. The weather gods did not hide the storm in an alternate universe and plan to drop it on us next Tuesday. The causes and conditions for the storm were not right, so it simply did not exist.

Or, to say it differently, "rainstorm" is just a label we use to point to a set of conditions. The rainstorm does not exist outside of its physical manifestations.

Under the right conditions, a particular sense of self is perceived to exist. With different causes and conditions, a different self is perceived. And under other conditions, no self is perceived. In this case, selfhood has not gone into hiding in an alternate universe. It has not gone to heaven or hell or been secreted away by the metaphysical forces or a mystical sleight of hand. It just doesn't exist.

The causes and conditions that give rise to a sense of self were described by the Buddha using the khandhas: tension, feeling tones, pointers and labels, a sense of solidity or continuity, concepts, stories, or disposition to color our experience with a self, and so on (pp. 167-176). These factors are amplified by the nervous system through homeostasis, homeostatic imbalance, etc. (pp. 179-198).

But when we relax deeply enough, all those conditions fade and we are left with anattā: nonself. It's the default — when the conditions aren't right, self doesn't go away: rather, it simply does not arise. When we are immersed in lovely music, quietly enjoying a sunset, lying in a field gazing into a starry night, there may not be enough tension, stories, and so forth to give rise to a perception of selfhood. It's just not relevant to our flow of experience and doesn't come to mind at that moment. Under different conditions, a sense of self does arise.

Again, this is not a metaphysical argument. It is a phenomenological description.

The Buddha never said the self does not exist at all. It obviously does. Anything created to express an idea does exist. Whether it exists in the world of experience is another matter. But the idea of self is useful. The conventional designation of a specific body, personal history, legal entity, developmental stages, etc., are all useful in specific circumstances. The Buddha agreed with all of that.

No "Higher" Self

There are just two forms of self to which the Buddha took exception. One is a so-called higher self, as an entity, essence, or soul. He said there is no self mysteriously outside conventional time and space and outside natural physical and mental processes. Andrew Olendzki puts it this way:

> *Self might be a useful word for referring to a person's body, feelings, perceptions, behavioral traits, and consciousness, but it cannot be construed as something underlying or transcending these manifestations … [A] person is not something other than how he or she manifests in experience.*[32]

Agency

The other common understanding of selfhood that the Buddha rejected was agency. He said there is no centralized,

---

[32] Andrew Olendzki, *Unlimiting Mind* (Wisdom Publications, 2012), p. 9.

consolidated, executive function that makes decisions and pulls the strings of physical and mental actions.

This rejection can be confusing because when we look inside, we can see thoughts, decisions, plans for actions, and other strategies. The Buddha agreed that all these are real and do happen.

He just said there is no entity running the show. Modern neuroscience agrees. As unintuitive as it feels, there seems to be no consolidated inner executive. In the brain, intelligence is distributive rather than centralized. There is thinking but no thinker, deciding but no decider, worrying but no worrier, planning but no planner.

Remember the *C. elegans* nematodes (p. 189), who won't feed alone when there is a nearby threat? They seem to be making decisions. But with only about three hundred neurons, nematodes have no mind and no meaningful sense of self, just blind instincts. We humans have many billions of neurons, so our minds are more complex. But we still have no central director only directing, no adjudicator only adjudicating.

Again, to quote Olendzki:

> *One can discern an executive function of intention or will, but there is no one to whom this belongs and no one who is wielding it.... [W]e go well beyond the data of experience to conclude from this phenomenology that there is a discrete entity identifiable as the self who is somehow "making" all these decisions.*[33]

A Useful Fiction

Nevertheless, in a lot of practical situations, the temporary fiction of selfhood is useful for sorting out social relationships, ethical responsibilities, and the like. For example, if due to

---

[33] Ibid, pp. 9-10.

inattention I run a red light and get a ticket, it is not legitimate for me to argue with the judge, "I am attentive now, therefore, that other self that ran the red light no longer exists. I should not be held responsible for what it did." To create a society that is supportive of deeper wellbeing, we have to start with behavioral norms that cultivate self-responsibility.

From a strictly biological perspective, people who believed they had a separate self to be protected were more likely to live long enough to pass on their genes. This is the "atta" or self view. Even if it is a delusion, evolution favors that view. It's been bred into us.

Cosmic Joke

Perhaps the universe has a sense of humor. Perhaps the Buddha did too, as seen in his famous half smile.

The goal of the Buddha's meditation seems to be to wake up completely through the cultivation of clearer and clearer awareness. As our meditation deepens, awareness does become purer and quieter. And then, just when it seems to approach perfect stillness, awareness disappears. The word "nirodha" or "cessation of awareness" refers to this. I call it "winking out." For a few moments (or maybe a long time) there is nothing. Not even a sense of the passage of time.

Perhaps invoking "clear awareness" was a joke because it seems to lead to no-awareness. From the outside, we look serene and often have the Buddha's half smile. But inside, there is nothing.

Another goal of the Buddha's meditation seems to be to see the self as it truly is. This is accomplished by clearing away misconceptions. As the last misconceptions fade, we expect that the true self will finally be visible. But when the last distortion dissipates, there is no self at all. Nothing. Anattā.

Were the instructions to see the self as it truly is some kind of joke? Were we supposed to know that clear awareness leads to non-awareness? And that finding our true self leads to nonself?

Or perhaps the Buddha had a different message in mind: these practices may not lead us where we think. If we truly show up, nirodha and anattā are not the end of the path. They are gateways to a whole different manner of unfolding. Rather than sitting in a noisy crowd of habits and gazing at peace in the distance, we find ourselves sitting in peace and watching the crowd of habits slowly drift away on their own.

Atta-Anattā: Self and Nonself

In our efforts to understand the Buddha's teachings, we may inadvertently overshoot the mark. He was never promoting a metaphysical principle. He merely said that the ways we try to name and mentally construct a sense of selfhood are confusing and misleading and not really supported by careful observation.

Perhaps the question is not: "Self versus nonself: which is right or wrong?" Perhaps a better question is: "In what ways is each view helpful?" Perhaps, like so many of the Buddha's teachings, atta-anattā turns out to be a middle way. Selfhood or non-selfhood is less something the world brings to us and more a way of perceiving (saññā khandha) and thinking (saṅkhāra khandha) that we inadvertently impose on the world. It's not something we see as much as a way of seeing.

I wake up in the morning and hear the birds singing enthusiastically, see a few tiny ants crawling through the bathroom sink in search of water, hear a rat scamper across the roof, and feel a cool, soft breeze come out of an endless blue sky.

If I bring a self view to this, I perceive an array of creatures and flora. Some seem supportive of me and some seem like pests. But each just wants to live its life in peace and wellbeing. And so do I. Through the self-view each creature seems unique and special and deserves kindness and generosity.

If I bring the nonself view to all this, I know that life on this planet started over three and a half billion years ago. The web of life itself —sometimes called "Gaia" — continues to emerge and evolve slowly in her own way. All of us are emersed in the ocean of life that includes Gandhi's "satyagraha" (which literally means "love force") and Thich Nhat Hanh's "interbeing" (each of us exists because all of us exist, and all of us exist because each of us exists). Each of us is but a tiny node of interbeing. We are fleeting physical manifestations of the all-ness of life. We arise, shine, and pass away like fireflies on a summer night. Through the anattā view we sense the wisdom of surrender into the sea of everything.

In these and other ways atta and anattā are not things life brings to us but modes of perception through which we view life.

When we look around at the specific issues in our world today, it strikes me that we need both views. We need the heart of kindness and generosity that welcomes the specialness of each organism. And we need the wisdom of satyagraha and interbeing that allows us to surrender into the ocean of life.

By themselves, they may not provide all the technical fixes for the issues of our time. But they generate the consciousness of atta-anattā that inspires new ways of engaging. This is not atta *versus* anattā, it is integration of selfhood *and* non-selfhood.

The self-only view sees each of us as arising and passing into oblivion. The strict nonself view sees the expanse of life but not individual creatures. The self/nonself view sees both at once and feels no conflict between them. There may be a gentle tension, but no essential difference. After all, they are not what the world brings to us, they are ways of viewing the world that we bring to it. Wisdom and heart are perfectly comfortable living together.

May it be so.

Self is not directly experienceable. If we look for a tangible experience, we may notice a gentle or not-so-gentle tightness. If we relax that tightness (turn toward, relax into, savor / smile), the sense of self thins out or fades away. This can be disconcerting, but that, too, is just another tightness that can be relaxed.

Refuges, Precepts, and Aspirations

Each morning before my first sitting, I recite the Buddha's refuges and precepts as well as the aspiration I mentioned at the end of Chapter 6. These embody much of what we've explored in this chapter and this book.

Refuges

I take refuge in the Buddha.
I take refuge in the Dhammā.
I take refuge in the Saṅgha.
For the second time
I take refuge in my good heart.
I take refuge in the natural unfolding of the mind-heart.
I take refuge in the community of fellow seekers,
those who have walked this path before me,
and the interdependence of beings.
For the third time
I take refuge in the Buddha.
I take refuge in the Dhammā.
I take refuge in the Saṅgha.

Precepts

I cultivate the precepts:
to be peaceful and refrain from harming intentionally;
to be content and
refrain from taking what is not given freely
to be attentive and refrain from sensory entanglement;
to truthful and
refrain from deceit, gossip,
harsh speech, and idle chatter;
to be simple and refrain from heedless intoxication;
to be kind and refrain from speaking or acting with ill will;
to be generous to myself and all beings.

Aspirations

Knowing that one day this body will cease
I seek simplicity, clarity, and acceptance,
and observe the mind-heart without preference.
When sending and receiving kindness feel the same,
self dissolves in contentment,
yearning fades into timeless presence,
and eternity merges with this moment right now.

15

Summary: Emerging Consciousness and Twilight Awareness

In the beginning was *not* the word. The Gospel of John got it wrong. Long before we had words, we had felt senses: hunger, thirst, loneliness, delight, ennui, pain, fear, joy, and more. From the perspective of evolution, words and language were a late development. Long before those arose in our ancient ancestors, there were feelings.

And in young humans today, feelings also arise long before words and language. Out of those feelings, consciousness surfaces. Consciousness and sense of self are like a wellspring that emerges from the depths that we can speculate about but cannot see.

Ideally, they evolve toward "twilight consciousness" — a quality of awareness I associate with being out in nature at twilight. It's more about feeling tone than words or language, more about mood than content, more about being present with what is than in trying to dictate what is present. I'm gently drawn to the natural presence around me: stars, deep blue sky, sun floating on the horizon, fields, trees, birds....

Twilight consciousness has neither self nor nonself. It's somewhere in between: a light self that I don't notice as it drifts into the distance. Similarly, a few thoughts float through, but I'm not paying attention to them either. They fade over the hillside.

This is no humdinger enlightenment, but simple contentment. The stars and sky and woods around me don't care whether I'm clear or deluded, feeling good or bad. And I don't care either. This is *not* the kind of not caring that turns away. Quite the opposite. It turns toward this moment with no urge to push or pull or direct anything. Things are just what they are, and that is enough. I notice a Buddha half smile at the corners of my mouth.

In preceding pages I've traced the complexities of how consciousness and a sense of self emerge from the unseen depths and, with a little presence, evolve toward twilight consciousness.

This concluding chapter is a short summary of this trajectory — a bird's eye view, if you will — of how consciousness and selfdom surface and evolve and some of their implications.

Consciousness Emerges

Consciousness and selfhood emerge from the necessity that living organisms must maintain homeostatic balances. Simple creatures do this reflexively — they rely on unconscious instincts. Complex creatures have more homeostatic balances to maintain, many of which will conflict with other homeostatic balances.

Rather than having built-in actions, we complex creatures have built-in feelings. They motivate us to move in various ways while giving us the freedom to choose which to act upon and in what order.

Consciousness is the internal space within which the various needs negotiate with one other in the context of the present environment. Sometimes we'll take advantage of opportunities that may not be at the top of the emotional needs list but are easy to meet right now.

This gives us free will: we can make choices. But our choices may be surrounded by feelings that push or pull us.

We can't choose whether or not these pushes and pulls are there. They are wired in. Emotions push us in various directions, so our choices are not purely intellectual. Competing drives play out in our feeling states. It's just that we have some choice as to whether to heed them or not — to succumb to their entreaties or to keep them at bay for the moment.

From the perspective of DNA reproducing itself in the coming generations, it doesn't matter if we're happy or depressed, wise or stupid, creative or destructive, generous or selfish, rich or poor. If those qualities help start the next generation, then they are more likely to live on. If not, they disappear from the evolutionary flow of life. Consciousness's prime purpose is to keep us alive long enough to create offspring with facsimiles of our DNA.

There are seven primordial affective emotions wired into mammals and birds.[34] They are the building blocks of all emotions and drives as well as of consciousness itself. When

---

[34] *Ibid*, Panksepp and Biven.

scientists surgically or chemically remove all seven affective emotions, consciousness and selfhood disappear: we go unconscious. This is not theoretical speculation; it's an empirical fact that has been demonstrated over and over. Consciousness grows out of primordial emotions which, in turn grow out of drives to maintain the homeostatic balances that we need to stay alive.

This connection between homeostasis, drives, primordial emotions, and consciousness is a crucial piece of the consciousness puzzle. The way they are linked together — from homeostasis to consciousness — may seem a little mind-boggling. But it is scientifically verifiable. Whether we understand it or not, whether it makes sense to us or not, it holds up to scientific scrutiny.

These emotions and drives focus on objects "out there" that can help restore homeostatic balances "in here." They focus on food, water, warmth, companionship, or whatever is needed from our surroundings.

But an unconscious or quasi-conscious by-product of this is a sense of self. If there is motivation to get something, this gives rise to a sense of self that carries those motivations. If there is wanting something that's missing or not wanting something that's present, the sense of self emerges that either wants it or wants to get rid of it. Attention doesn't focus on the self that's looking for food, entertainment, friendship, shelter, or whatever. Yet self quietly arises inside. It flexes its muscles, so to speak, even as it stays in the background.

Notice that the self does not create these drives and emotions. The drives and emotions create the sense of self.

No Self, No Suffering

In Buddhist circles, greed, hatred and delusions are said to be the source of suffering. And there is some obvious truth to this. But there is a subtlety that is sometimes missed. Getting rid of greed and hatred, wanting and not wanting, desire and aversion is not an option so long as we live in an organic body that must maintain homeostatic balances. These drives keep us alive. If we stop taking care of them, we will die sooner rather than later. Remember Ava, Bea, and Cindy (pp. 89-92)? Our genes will be removed from the gene pool.

So the solution is not to get rid of the emotions and their attendant drives. The solution is much subtler: relax the identification with those emotions and drives. The feelings will still be there. There will still be flow of consciousness with feelings, images, and thoughts. But there will be no self that owns them. That self is a fiction created by the saññā khandha, the perception aggregate (see pp. 171-172). It's a metaphorically convenient way to talk about drives and needs.

So rather than focus on the needs and drives or their objects, we can focus on the sense of self itself — the supposed carrier of all those drives. And we do this until it becomes very clear that that self is just a metaphor — a poetic tool for conceptualizing experience. But it distorts perception when we hang on to it.

Self is an illusion created by strong (or mild) drives and feeling tones. When we look at it more clearly, it starts to evaporate like soap bubbles. The Buddha put it this way:

> *The body's like a ball of foam,*
> *And feeling is like a bubble,*
> *Perception is like a mirage,*
> *Constructs are like a pith-less tree,*
> *And consciousness is just a trick.*
>
> – Samyutta Nikaya 22.95

Again: *getting rid of* the emotions and drives is not an option as long as we are in living bodies and want to stay alive. Rather, it is the *breaking identification with* the emotions and drives and their proxy — the sense of self — that is helpful. That is where the deeper spiritual work bears fruit. If we don't identify with those feelings or sense of self, then there is no self to suffer.

Consciousness creates the space within which it is possible to see those feelings without identifying with them, a space in which the negotiations can take place. But it's the loss of identification with them that brings freedom.

Our identification can be strong. Relaxing it is not a simple or easy task. We can't will it away. Will just creates more density and identification with the self that seems to be doing the willing.

Rather, it is through the relaxation, opening, and seeing what is most deeply true that we realize there is no one holding those feelings. It's a flow of consciousness, not a flow of self. If there is no identification, there is no self.

It's like the weather — when the causes and conditions of a storm are not present, the storm does not exist. It doesn't hide away in some altered dimension. It just doesn't arise. Without identification, the causes and conditions of suffering get no foothold. They cease to exist. Without them there is no sense of self. And without a sense of self, there is just a flow of experience without anyone or anything to suffer.

The simple contentment of twilight consciousness is freedom for each of us.

The Energy Costs of Freedom

But that freedom comes with costs, some of which are hard to see.

In order to negotiate between the organism (us) and the outer world, it helps to be attuned to what's going on inside. It helps to be present and mindful. At the same time, to successfully negotiate, it helps to remember lessons from past experience about what has worked before. At the very least it helps to have a CliffsNotes summary of the most salient points.

So consciousness must negotiate between the present-moment reality and past realities. It must realistically assess "here and now" guided by "there and then." There can be tension between that which has been learned from past events as contrasted with current events.

Complex organisms such as humans and other mammals create inner models of the world around them and the world within themselves and allow these to interact in our thoughts and imaginations (as we saw in Chapters 9 and 10). That allows us to be creative and to try new things mentally, with less risk of immediate demise if we miscalculate. We have a chance to work it out in our minds before committing to a course of action in the physical world. It helps us survive long enough to reproduce.

But it also uses up a lot of energy. As noted in Chapter 9 (p. 121), the human brain uses about 20 percent of the body's energy while comprising only about 2 percent of its weight. The brain is expensive. We must also spend years maturing such a complex nervous system. It takes longer for humans to reach adulthood than it does most other animals. That means we need even more energy to support our survival until we can grow up and reproduce.

Other organisms use less energy creating these complex neural pathways. They survive using more unconscious instincts and less processing of present and past memories. We trade all this in for flexibility — the capacity to adapt more quickly to rapidly changing situations. It gives us more freedom.

For the most part, we like our big brains. While we think we are the best the world has produced, it's humbling to realize that homo sapiens have only been around for a few hundred thousand years. Our ancestor hominids got started a few million years earlier. Cockroaches, on the other hand, have been around for 280 million years. They predate the dinosaurs. They were crawling around as dinosaurs arose and passed away. From the perspective of evolutionary survival, it will take us hundreds of millions of years to catch up with cockroaches.

I came of age during the 1960s. I'm a white, slightly overeducated, middle-class American. Among my peers there was a belief that liberal democratic values and ever-more-sophisticated science could move us onward and upward forever.

More recently, doubt has begun to seep in: the threat of ecological collapse, political gridlock, blatant wars of aggression, degradation of the value of speaking the truth, and more. Some now worry that we humans might destroy the world.

Rest assured, we can't. We can make it incapable of supporting human life. But nature and the world can get along without us. The cockroaches are likely to still be here even if we kill ourselves off. Life in some form can go on without us.

Be that as it may, most of us humans would like to use our complex, self-reflective consciousnesses to do more than survive and breed. We'd like to feel better, happier, wiser, and more content. We have a deepening understanding that our wellbeing is intimately tied to the survival of other humans and other species. We'd like to use our brains and hearts and imagination to evolve a world where health, happiness, contentment, and wellbeing are part of the mix. To do this we need a consciousness that is more inclusive.

This is where meditation and other spiritual practices can lend a hand. They help us to see beyond baseline survival by realizing how deeply the fates of all of us are tied together. In the collective contentment of emerging twilight consciousness is freedom for all of us.

Appendices

Appendix A

The Six Rs

While meditating, sooner or later, a distraction completely hijacks our attention. These distractions are called "hindrances" (*nīvaraṇa* in Pāli). We may not even see them coming: one moment we're peaceful, the next we're rehearsing a conversation, planning our day, reminiscing about yesterday, or attending to something other than this moment.

The drifting mind is a symptom of tension. This side of enlightenment, we all have many tensions. The distraction points to where the tightness resides. The trick is to release it wisely. Self-criticism creates even more tension, as does buckling down and trying harder.

A better approach is a six-phased process called "the Six Rs," which was developed by Bhante Vimalaraṁsi and his students.

Another good approach is the Three Essential Practices, as described in Chapter 5 (pp. 59-66). These are a practical implementation of the first three of the Buddha's so-called Four Noble Truths.

The advantage of the Six Rs is that they are hardy and can be used anytime the mind is disturbed, no matter how chaotic. The advantage of the Three Practices is that when the mind is peaceful, the Six Rs can feel clunky and distracting. The Three Practices and the Six Rs are completely compatible. They both skillfully guide the mind-heart back to its natural peacefulness.

I mostly use the Three Practices. But the Six Rs are a good backup for those times when the mind-heart is particularly stormy.

Recognize

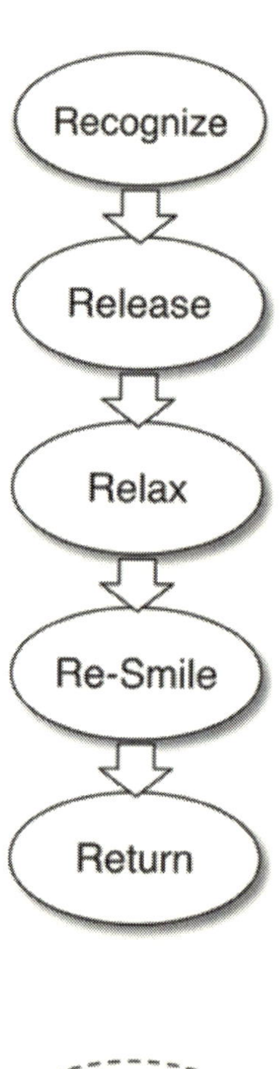

The first step in the Six Rs is Recognizing that our attention has moved away from the primary object of meditation. The ability to observe how the mind's awareness shifts from one thing to another is crucial. In time it will be clear that something specific drew us to that particular distraction, though the reason may not be clear now. That's fine. If a thought drew us away, there's no need to get involved in its content. If the content of a thought could wake us up, we would have awakened a long time ago. Instead, we notice the feeling in the mind-heart. There will be some tension: worry, curiosity, aversion, fear, desire, doubt, or some other attitude.

Recognizing this tightness on its own terms is very helpful. We want to recognize sensations as sensations, feelings as feelings, and thoughts as thoughts rather than confusing a thought or label with a sensation or feeling.

Release

The second step is to Release the hindrance. Our culture has a bias toward fixing things or getting them under control. The Six-R practice is the opposite. We just let the distraction be without trying to change it. If we're upset, we don't indulge the turmoil or try to squelch it. We just notice, "Ah, there is a lot of hurt and anger in my system." If we notice daydreaming about an imagined vacation, we don't go off into the fantasy or try to shut it down. We just notice that daydreaming is happening.

As Suzuki Roshi put it, "The best way to control a cow is to put it in a large pasture." Release means giving the distraction some space. It may wander across the pasture and out of our lives. Or it may come back and stare us in the face with big brown eyes. Either is just fine.

Releasing isn't pushing the distraction away. It's just letting go of our grip on it. To truly let something be means it can do what it wants. We no longer hold it close or hold it off. The best way to control a cow is to Release it into a large pasture and let the cow be a cow.

Relax

The third phase is to Relax. The first two phases are passive: we Recognize the distraction and Release it or let it be. In this third phase, we start to act. This action is directed inward — soothing our stress by softening the tension in it. We aren't trying to change the hindrance or our thoughts or feelings. We aren't trying to Relax the distraction; we merely Release it to do what it wants. We look inside, notice any physical, mental, or emotional tensions, and Relax them. That's all. The term the Buddha used was dramatic: he said "abandon" the tension. Walk away from it. We don't have to search for tension like an enthusiastic detective. Just Relax. That's enough.

There's no need to force relaxation. It is just a gentle invitation — like a sigh. Yet this opportunity to Relax physically, emotionally, and mentally is very helpful!

Re-Smile

The next phase is to invite a lighter state of mind. One way to do this is to smile — not a forced smile but a gentle, sincere one. A frown takes more energy and results in tension. So, as we Relax, smiling comes easily.

It's called "Re-smile" because we do it over and over (and because we needed another "R" word). But in truth, Re-smiling refers to any uplifted state — lightness, kindness, joy, ease, gratitude, spaciousness, or any quality with little tension in it.

Sometimes this lightness comes by acknowledging, "Boy, that situation sure has me by the throat. Cool." It helps to take ourselves lightly.

The smile may be on our lips, in our mind, in our eyes, or in our heart. If no uplifted state comes on its own, we raise the corners of the mouth slightly. Even if we do this mechanically, it neurologically encourages the brain to lighten up. Having a good sense of humor about how the mind drifts is helpful.

Return

Now we take the relaxed mind-heart and this brighter, lighter quality back to radiating happiness and wellbeing or just resting in equanimity. We Return our attention to our base meditation practice.

Repeat

The final phase is to Repeat the process whenever it's needed and as often as it's needed. This step does not flow automatically from the preceding Rs. But it is included as a reminder that we may need to use the Six Rs a lot. During meditation, if distractions keep grabbing our awareness, it is not a problem if we Six-R each time. Meditation is not about sustaining any particular state. States come and go. Meditation is about seeing how attention moves. By six-R'ing, we see the mind-heart's movements more and more clearly.

If one or several uses of the Six Rs didn't release all the tension, it will let us know by arising again. We Recognize, Release, Relax, Re-smile, and Return again, perhaps going a little further each time.

That is the beauty of this process. We don't have to do it perfectly. Doing it just a little is good enough. As we Repeat, it gradually works itself out.

Rolling the Rs

The first five Rs are not separate from one another. As we learn this process, the Rs begin to merge together. Rather than remaining isolated steps, they become a dynamic flow of energy.

To Recognize a hindrance clearly, we naturally step back from it a little. "Let's have a look at this," implies getting a little distance so we can see it clearly. Stepping back is part of the Release. As we Release, we tend to Relax. As we Relax, our mood brightens. From this brighter place, we naturally Return to radiating wellbeing or resting in peacefulness.

Think of this as "rolling the Rs." Don't push for this flow, but don't be surprised if the stages start to flow together naturally into a single process with multiple phases: Recognize-Release-Relax-Re-smile-Return.

Appendix B

Spectrum of Awareness

The Spectrum of Awareness charts the transformation of the mind-heart as it expands and relaxes. Consciousness shifts from the objects or contents of awareness to the field of awareness itself and beyond. The sense of self evolves from feeling like a solid entity to feeling like a mist evaporating in the morning sun. The Spectrum was introduced in Chapter 4 (pp. 49-58). Table 4, below, and offers specific references to complete descriptions of each phase.

Table 4: Spectrum of Awareness

Phase	Examples (and references to fuller descriptions)
1 Content	Plans, stories, ideas, problems, friends, foes (see "Content Fades into Processes," p. 76).
2 Processes	Thinking, worrying, storytelling, figuring, planning, arguing, daydreaming (see "Process Fades into Qualities of Awareness," p. 77).
3 Qualities of Awareness	Clear, foggy, agitated, calm, fast, sluggish, sticky, spacious, open, tight ("Qualities Fade into Field of Awareness," p. 77).
4 Field of Awareness	Noticing awareness apart from its content, process, qualities, or textures (see "Blank Spots," p. 81).
5 Nothingness	Emptiness, "winking out," nirodha, nibbāna.

Appendix C

Awareness, Intelligence, and Consciousness

It is helpful to distinguish between three different terms: "consciousness," "awareness," and "intelligence." They are often used interchangeably. But I use them to distinguish three distinct faculties.

For example, I look out the window and see a clear sky and a man in shorts walking a dog down the street.

Awareness

Awareness is the faculty that knows what I'm seeing: the sky, a man in shorts, a dog, and so forth. Notice that without memory, moment-to-moment awareness is not helpful. If, when I look back inside, I've forgotten all that I just saw, awareness is useless.

Intelligence

Intelligence goes beyond awareness. It is the capacity to deduce things I have not perceived directly. I deduce that it is a warm day, that I don't need a jacket when I go out, and so on. Intelligence helps us figure things out.

Intelligence also relies on memory of facts that are considered "common knowledge." For example, people wear shorts when it's warm and jackets when it's cold.

High-speed computers can have more memory capacity and faster calculation speed than humans. Artificial intelligence depends on these expanded capabilities. But they are not conscious.

Consciousness

Consciousness is more difficult to pin down. It's easier to say what it's not: it's not awareness nor is it intelligence. These play a secondary role in consciousness, but it's neither of those.

Consciousness seems to have something to do with self-awareness, or awareness of being an object in the world. But it's more than that. In 1974, the philosopher Thomas Nagel wrote an article called "What Is It Like to Be a Bat?" He argued that we can recognize consciousness in a creature when we can say what it might be like to be that creature. This harkens back to my childhood musings of wondering what it would be like to view the world through the eyes of my cat, a bird, or another person.

The scientist and philosopher Anil Seth suspects that consciousness is not even possible without at least a dim sense of self. This rings true to me. But suspicions, "ringing true," and answers to the questions of what it's like to be something are fuzzy, imprecise, and not very satisfying for me.

Another approach to the question is to ask, "What's consciousness made of?" "What are its ingredients?" This is where we started in Chapter 2.

Appendix D

The Hard Problem Revisited

When we meditate, we are in the soup of awareness and consciousness. They seem to arise out of the gray matter inside our skulls — out of our brains. But how do brains do that? How does awareness arise out of neural activity? How does consciousness emerge from anatomical structures?

It's a simple, elemental, and totally baffling question. For hundreds of years, scientists and philosophers have pondered: How does objective physical matter create subjective, immaterial experience? As I mentioned in Chapter 11, in the early 1990s the Australian philosopher David Chalmers dubbed this "the Hard Problem." At that time we didn't have a clue about where to start answering it.

In contrast, we've made great progress with the so-called "easy problem": how do physiological processes correlate with subjective experience? We can insert probes deep into the brain and give tiny electrical shocks to various regions. If the patient is conscious, she or he will report the image of a butterfly, the memory of a childhood pet, the awareness of an upwelling of fear or anger, or other pictures or emotions.

We have mapped the various kinds of experiences that arise in various parts of the brain. We can show correlations between objective stimuli and subjective experiences.

But why this works — why specific areas of the brain give rise to specific experiences — has been a confoundingly hard problem to address until recently. Today we are closer to answers. We may have most of the pieces in place for tracing the origins of consciousness to biological processes and back even farther to fundamental laws of physics.

The Hard Hard Problem

Behind the Hard Problem is what could be called "the Hard Hard Problem," which is: "How does a subjectively 'solid' sense of a self arise out of nothing?"

The assumption behind that question — that there is no solid, enduring self — may seem obscure or as esoteric as asking, "How many angels can dance on the head of a pin?" But it has a very practical context.

The Buddha was interested in alleviating human suffering. He solved the problem not by eliminating suffering but by eliminating "the sufferer" — or at least identification with a self. If there is no sufferer, then there is no suffering. So these inquiries have practical, nitty-gritty applications, even if they do not solve the Hard Problem or the Hard Hard Problem.

Acknowledgments and Bibliography

They say it takes a village to raise a child. Yet it may take more than that to write a book. As I look through these pages and see all the obvious and subtle influences on my understanding, I am humbled and grateful for the interdependent web of colleagues, students, and friends who have shaped its contents. This writing is an inadequate representation of their collective wisdom. To the extent that my understanding has fallen short or been in error, I apologize and hope that you, dear reader, have been able to separate the wheat from the chaff.

My main dhammā mentors in the last ten or fifteen years include John Travis of Mountain Stream and Bhante Vimalaraṁsi of Dhammā Sukha Meditation Center. In my early years of practice there was Larry Rosenberg of the Cambridge (Massachusetts) Insight Meditation Center. In over fifty residential retreats of ten days or longer, there are a vast array of teachers, mentors, and therapists who have nudged, moved, or inspired me in ways I can see reflected in these chapters. This includes the Thai Forest meditation master Ajahn Tong, who guided a six-week retreat in Southeast Asia.

There are also many teachers and scholars whom I never met outside the contents of their writings. Of particular impact on this book are:

- Tara Brach, *Radical Acceptance* (New York: Bantam Books, 2003)
- Ben Connelly, *Vasubandhu's "Three Natures": A Practitioner's Guide for Liberation* (Somerville, Massachusetts: Wisdom Publications, 2022)
- Antonio Damasio, *Self Comes to Mind: Constructing the Conscious Brain* (New York: Vintage Books, 2021) and *Feeling and Knowing: Making Minds Conscious* (New York: Pantheon Books, 2021)
- Eugene T. Gendlin, *Focusing* (New York: Bantam Books, 1978, 1981)
- Donald Hoffman, *The Case Against Reality: Why Evolution Hid the Truth from our Eyes* (New York: W. W. Norton and Company, 2019)
- Kumāra Bhikkhu, *What You Might Not Know about Jhāna and Samādhi* (Creative Commons Attribution-NonCommercial-NoDerivs (CC BY-NC-ND) 3.0 Unported License, 2022)
- Andrew Olendzki, *Unlimiting Mind: The Radical Experiential Psychology of Buddhism* (Somerville, Massachusetts: Wisdom Publications, 2012) and *Unlimiting Mind: The Radically Experimental Psychology of Buddhism* (Somerville, Massachusetts: Wisdom Publications, 2010)
- Jaak Panksepp and Lucy Biven, *The Archaeology of Mind: Neuroevolutionary Origins of Human Emotions* (New York: W. W. Norton and Company, 2012)
- Anil Seth, *Being You: A New Science of Consciousness* (New York: Dutton, 2021)
- Mark Solms, *The Hidden Spring: A Journey to the Source of Consciousness* (New York: W. W. Norton & Company, 2021)
- Khenpo Tsultrim Gyamtso Rinpoche and Lama Shenpen Hookham. *Progressive Stages of Meditation on Emptiness* (Criccieth, Wales: Shrimala Trust, 2016)
- The writings of Karl Friston and many others

Also impacting this book are many of my students and Dhammā friends. Several read the manuscript and made valuable suggestions and comments including Prashant

Billore, Bret Brown, David Johnson, Judy Bell, Liam McClintock, Richard Maddock, to name a few. I am also grateful to my editors, Daia Gerson and Susan Piperato.

And last but not least is Erika, my wife of over fifty years who, among many other things, read and commented on the manuscript through several iterations.

Topic Index

Note: **bold page numbers indicate primary entries.**

* Each of these seven primary affective emotions also have detailed listing found under their own names elsewhere in this index.

S

Made in the USA
Middletown, DE
11 March 2023